MISSION LIBERIA

MISSION LIBERIA

The War Could Not Stop Us

Brian J. Knightley

Brian J. Knightley O.F.

Matador
5 Weir Road
Kibworth Beauchamp
Leicester LE8 0LQ, UK
Tel: 0116 279 2299
Fax: 0116 279 2277
Email: books@troubador.co.uk
Web: www.troubador.co.uk/matador

ISBN 978 184876-468-2

British Library Cataloguing in Publication Data.
A catalogue record for this book is available from the British Library.

Printed in Great Britain by the MPG Books Group, Bodmin and King's Lynn

Matador is an imprint of Troubador Publishing Ltd

This book is dedicated to
Major Inger Merit Nygård *who gave us great encouragement*
and to the ***Norwegian Salvation Army****, who together with the*
Norwegian government *provided the funds for many of*
our major projects in Liberia.
Also;
in gratitude to ***Tony Hage*** *who,*
as well as finding land for us to build on,
was also a true friend opening up his home
when we needed somewhere to stay and coming to our
rescue many times when we were caught in situations
that were beyond our means to cope with on our own.

ACKNOWLEDGEMENTS

This book could not have been written without the total support and encouragement of Dorothy, my wife. Not only was she one of the most insistent that it should be written, but was also the greatest help in bringing it to completion. She has spent hours reading and rereading it, not only to make corrections but also to add many of the incidents of interest I had left out.

Major Rosemary Dawson deserves a special word of gratitude too, for using her editorial skills in the final preparation of the book, and the hours she generously gave to proof reading it.

My thanks also go to many other people who have told me that the book should be written. To all of them I offer my sincere thanks, with apologies for keeping them waiting so long.

The Author with Dorothy, his wife, and Ernest, their adopted Liberian son.
(Photograph taken on a return visit – November 2006)

CONTENTS

FOREWORD

I do hope that the readers of this book will find encouragement by hearing what was achieved against all odds. We arrived in Liberia with one suitcase each, hand luggage with our Bibles and a cornet. We didn't have a lot of money; certainly not enough to start meeting much of the physical and material need that was obvious all around us. But we had come with a strong faith to share and believed that we had been called to our mission by God with confidence he would meet our need for resources.

The greatest resource needed was human. There were no other expatriate colleagues to assist us, but quickly God did supply willing workers. Along with newly trained officers God gave us eager, born-again youths who were ready to work hard to spread the Gospel. As a consequence, The Salvation Army developed in Liberia as a very youthful movement and where, unusually, the men outnumbered the women.

It was the Command Mission Team, made up of young men willing to dare for Christ that really took The Salvation Army Church out of Monrovia for the first time in earnest since the civil war reached the city. They then began to spread its influence in all directions from the capital. It was a fact that the rebels who were destroying and killing were mostly young men.

However, it was equally true that those working under The Salvation Army's direction, seeking to bring Christ to the people of Liberia, were also in their teens and early twenties. They also risked their lives on behalf of their leader, Jesus Christ, to take His message of love to the people.

The Salvation Army Church in Liberia is made up of many tribes and that is also reflected in our officer ranks. As you read this book you will also see that progress has been made on all fronts: The Salvation Army has reached half the counties, our schools compete with the very best in Liberia whilst still giving sound Bible teaching, and it will not be long before our first Salvation Army sponsored doctor will graduate.

Now I would thank those who have kept reminding me to "write that book!!" I hope you will enjoy it and that it will inspire you to attempt the impossible for God. Looking back, in the midst of a civil war, I believe God enabled us to do exactly that.

B.J.K.

LIBERIA WEST AFRICA

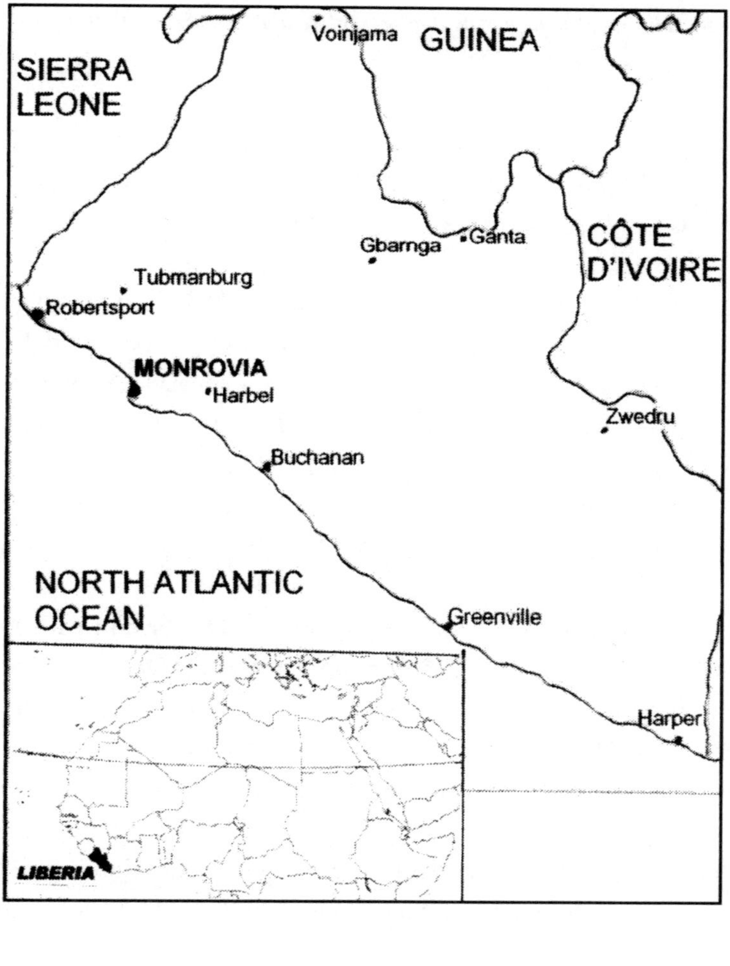

LIBERIA IN BRIEF

A little background knowledge of the nation of Liberia is helpful to the understanding of some events that took place and experiences that my wife and I had in Liberia.

Liberia is on the west coast of Africa between Sierra Leone and Côte D'Ivoire; what was formerly known as the 'Grain Coast' because of its production of hot 'Grains of Paradise'.

It began to develop as a nation in 1822 with the settlement of freed slaves from the US and by 1847 it had become a republic; the first in all of Africa! The Americo-Liberians, known as Congo's, gradually became dominant and ruled continuously until in 1980, when a military coup, led by Master Sergeant Samuel Doe, ushered in a decade of rule by indigenous Liberians; most of whom were drawn from President Doe's Krahn tribe.

In late December, 1989 Charles Taylor began a rebellion with an army known as the NPFL★. Though very successful at first, he was thwarted for a long time both by the tenacity of the national army (the AFL), and also by the factionalising of his army when Prince Johnson broke away and formed the INPFL★. Another two armies, known as ULIMO K★ & ULIMO J★, also began to seek power. When President Doe was killed, the fighting still continued between the forces of the AFL★, NPFL★ and both ULIMO factions.

After the loss of many lives and the looting of much of Liberia, elections were held in 1997 which made Charles Taylor the nation's President. However, almost immediately, various other armies developed in opposition to Taylor; LURD* in the north and north-west and MODEL* in the east. LURD was led by leaders who were ardently Muslim, and one of the political aims of their organization was, initially, to set up an Islamic state (see appendix 2). However, many of its fighters were simply opposed to Taylor and were not Muslims so there never was an Islamic takeover of the government. Eventually, in 2003, to save the complete destruction of Monrovia and ignominious defeat, Taylor was forced to resign and enter exile in Nigeria. He is now being tried in The Hague for war crimes which include the use of child soldiers and the sale of arms to Sierra Leone for 'blood' diamonds.

With the resignation of Taylor in 2003 and his exile to Nigeria, the civil war was ended with the help of a strong contingent of UN peacekeepers (UNMIL*). In 2005 democratic elections were held, and the final runoff between Ellen Johnson Sirleaf and George Weah (Liberia's most famous footballer) ended in victory for Ellen Johnson Sirleaf with a 20% majority. Now, with the presence of at least 15,000 UN troops, the country has been slowly recovering from the trauma of civil war but the economy is at rock bottom and the peace is fragile.

Liberians are proud of the fact that they are the oldest republic in the Africa and have never been colonized though it is a fact that the freed slaves for a long time held all the power and most of the best land. Liberia now has the added 'first' of being the first African state to have a woman president. In the same way that African countries colonized by Britain tend to look to the UK for the basis of their laws, the judiciary, governance, policing and education, the Liberians have looked to base their systems on those found in the US.

There are 16 major tribes with different languages though some, like the Kpelle and Gola, are very close. However, about 20% speak English which is the official lingua franca and is the one used in all schools. Almost 60% can read and write elementary English though there is a 7:4 split in favour of males. Christians outnumber Muslims 2 to 1 but there are many (probably equal to the number of Christians) who are neither. These are those who still practice the indigenous religions based mostly on ancestral spirit worship, together with subtle varieties of Pantheism. Even many Christians and Muslims still have tendencies to be drawn back into superstitious practices when faced with drastic situations. One quite big cause for concern to the churches is the problems posed by the secret societies. The most prominent of these are the Sande (females) found predominantly with Bassa people and the Poro (males) found mostly with Gola and Kpelle tribes people. Some tribes do not have secret societies which are believed to have been introduced by the Mende speaking people many years ago. These secret societies do have many good aspects to them, for they teach good behaviour and respect (particularly to their elders) and also impart traditional knowledge of farming and hunting. However, female mutilation is carried out by the Sande and some superstitious beliefs are indoctrinated into them along with some pagan practices. It used to be that adolescents were taken off into the bush for three or four years by a 'devil' (a man on stilts, wearing a mask) to be given this training, but nowadays this is usually reduced to three of four months in order not to interfere too much with normal education.

Liberia has a hot equatorial climate, with heavy rains from the middle of April to the end of October. During the rest of the year it gets very hot and dry. Harmattan winds, with sand from the Sahara, add to the discomfiture of the heat and humidity. It does get colder in the low mountain area to the north-east. Much of the coastline is characterized by lagoons, mangrove swamps and river-deposited sandbars.

During the war the rain forests suffered considerable deforestation for which the majority of inhabitants gained little profit. Its natural resources are iron ore, coal, timber, diamonds, gold and hydropower. Most of the land was originally covered with tropical rain forests but large expanses have now been cut down and turned over to the cultivation of rubber trees which includes the Firestone rubber plantations; once the largest in the world. At present the processing of rubber is the main industry. Apart from palm oil processing, timber and diamonds trades there is little industry at present. In the field of agriculture rubber, coffee, cocoa, rice, cassava, palm oil, sugar cane, bananas and timber are the main products but some goats and sheep are brought over the Guinea border for the home market. Throughout the civil conflict the use of the Liberian flag for shipping registration continued and even now still brings a large sum into the nation's exchequer. Since the war the Liberia Agricultural Company (LAC) has been granted huge concessionary rights over land in Grand Bassa. Though the work opportunities have been welcomed, the relocating of the indigenous people and the destruction of their homes in the district has not been received well and led, in September 2007, to the killing of the manager, Mr. Bruno Michael.

Before the war there were two railroads leading to the two major sources of iron ore; at Bong and in the Nimba hills to the north of the country. In 2005 LAMCO was given the concession for the Nimba ore fields which they had mined before the civil war. Tenders are currently being offered for those in Bong (and two other nearby fields). There is reported to be more iron ore in Liberia than any other African state and that it could possibly have the seventh largest reserves of coal in the world.

In the days before Doe's coup Liberia did not have its own currency but exclusively used the US currency. Doe introduced Liberia's own coins and notes which slowly depreciated. Now the US dollar and the Liberian dollar are both in circulation at an exchange rate of US$1 to L$70. Usually a slightly higher rate is obtainable for large value US$ notes.

Possibly because the Liberian people have never been colonized, there are few racial problems. A Westerner is not resented but neither is he given any special treatment. In spite of the civil war the ordinary Liberian doesn't seem to have any deep-seated hatred for other tribes, even though at times the fighting took on a very ethnic and tribal nature. In Salvation Army corps, the members and the officers come from a wide variety of the tribes and work well together. It has been a great help to us that the lingua franca is English, because this has enabled us to send our officers to any tribal area with the expectation that there will always be someone who could translate for them.

***Armed Militia**

AFL: Armed Forces of Liberia - Leader: Various

NPFL: National Patriotic Front of Liberia - Leader: Charles Taylor

INPFL: Independent NPFL - Leader: Prince Johnson

ULIMO - J: United Liberation Movement of Liberia for Democracy – Leader: Roosevelt Johnson

ULIMO – K: United Liberation Movement of Liberia for Democracy – Leader: Alhaji Kromah
LURD: Liberians United for Reconciliation and Democracy
MODEL: Movement for Democracy in Liberia

Peace Keepers

ECOMOG: Economic Community of West African States Monitoring Group
UNMIL: United Nations Mission in Liberia

CHAPTER 1

A Challenging Appointment

Four o'clock on Easter Saturday morning, April 6, 1996. The sound was deafening. At first, in our rude awaking, we thought it was the sudden breaking of a tropical storm. But this was no act of God. This was man at his worst. The war was on again and this time it was starting outside our compound.

There was beating on our door with desperate cries for it to be opened. Jackson and Samuel had been sleeping on the upstairs veranda when things had erupted in the road. Being so close to the noise of rockets, mortars and heavy machine guns was an awesome experience. We let the boys in, grabbed some clothes and hurried downstairs. We knew that with a concrete floor above us we would be better protected from rockets and mortars than by the flimsy asbestos roof. The boys dived under the table and Dorothy and I sat in the cupboard under the stairs. Not for long though – our four dogs insisted in joining us, and then competed to be the one closest to Dorothy.

We had been in Liberia for four-and-a-half years during which time the civil war had raged around Monrovia and occasionally within it. The sound of gunfire was not new to us. This time, though, we had to face the possibility that a mortar or a rocket might bring our term in Liberia to a dramatic conclusion. But right from the beginning of our time in Liberia we were fully aware that the dangers were real. We had entered into our calling with our eyes open, knowing the risks. It would be wrong to say that we had no fear, but it is true that it was something that was never overwhelming. Our faith had been put to the test in many ways, and even in the most near-death situations had never been found wanting.

It is true that even when we had first been invited to take up our appointment in Liberia, things were not good in that country. Charles Taylor's rebel forces had not reached Monrovia, though they were quite close. Unfortunately, three days before we were scheduled to arrive in the city defences were breached and rebels took over the last remaining airstrip. We had been tantalizingly close to getting into the country but had to accept it was not to be. God knew best and our time had not yet come.

Our predecessor, Major Len Millar, who had been waiting to hand over to us, had exited in haste from the country in almost the last civilian plane to leave Monrovia before the airport was closed. The rebels had broken through the outer city defences and had stormed into Monrovia as far as the City Hall.

We now had to wait a frustrating seventeen months before any planes were flying into Monrovia. During that time we worked at our International Headquarters and helped with the International Congress which was being held in London. After five months, however, at our request, we had an interview with the International Secretary for Africa. Surely, we said, there must be somewhere in Africa where we could be usefully employed while we wait for Liberia to open up? There were two places, we were told: one was a financial role in Zaire, the other a public relations role in Zambia. I had only the slightest knowledge of double entry book-keeping and a failed 'O' level in French, so I decided that the PR role was the preferred one – just! Dorothy agreed, and she was given duties in the projects office.

Back in 1980, just three weeks before full independence was celebrated in Zimbabwe, we had taken up our first overseas appointment in that country. We started as the Salisbury City Corps officers but within ten months, at our request, moved out of the city to run a secondary boarding mission school at Bradley; almost fifty miles from the nearest town, Bindura. Our experiences in Zimbabwe will have to be the subject of another book but I mention it because when we went to Zambia, formerly known as Northern Rhodesia, we expected to find a similarly beautiful country. Sadly, this was not so. Salisbury (now Harare) was then a fine looking city with its attractive and wide avenues lined with jacaranda trees. In season, their blossoms covered the streets with a mauve or crimson carpet. There were parks, with tea shops where we used to relax with a toasted sandwich or a fancy cake. The shopping centre had stores almost as grand as those back home in Oxford Street, though I have to admit that there were times when some foods were in short supply. Fortunately we had arrived there just as the embargo on fuel was lifted and the coupons we were given on arrival were never used.

So we set off for Zambia, expecting to find Lusaka like the picture of Salisbury that we still had in our minds. What we found was very different. Clearly it had seen better days. The buildings were not so different from those in Zimbabwe, but were dilapidated; needing repair and redecorating. There was a depressing air about the place, as well as a strong smell. Some of this was a result of a common practice of filling the many pot holes in the roads with rubbish; often bad vegetables and fruit. Even the parks, inside the city and out, were generally lacking in care and had lost their former glory of colonial days. The truth was, the country had given so much of its wealth in supporting refugees and freedom fighters from Zimbabwe it was now almost bankrupt. Even the copper mines, which had provided so much of its former wealth, had mostly become too uneconomical to mine. Now, almost twenty years later, I believe the high price of metals has given these mines and the surrounding towns a new lease of life.

I have to admit I wasn't wonderfully successful as a public relations man but I do believe that I had some influence on the youth at the corps. It was they who helped me to remember that I was an ordained minister of the gospel.

This year, sixteen years after leaving Zambia, I was encouraged to receive a letter from one of these young men, Cidiq. He is now in the States, and successfully making his way on the pop religious music scene. He had found my name whilst browsing the net and had contacted our London HQ to find my address. After rejoicing that he had found me, he continued giving a summary of his life to date. How could I not be moved when he concluded saying; "*You became the first man to ever show me fatherly love, and in my heart you became my father, always have been and always will. To this day I still do not understand why you cared enough to want to help me change and become what God wanted me to be.*" Since leaving Zambia I had wondered why God had led us to go to Zambia. At least now I have received one very good reason.

Every day in Zambia we searched for news about Liberia. We learned that several of the West Africa countries had sent a combined force into Liberia, known as ECOMOG. They had managed to drive the rebels out of Monrovia and the surrounding areas but did not attempt to attack Taylor in the interior. Inside the city President Samuel Doe was captured by the leader of a breakaway rebel faction and brutally murdered. The politicians who had not fled Monrovia then set up an interim government, which had no real influence over anything outside of the city.

At last news reached us that a small plane was flying in and out of the capital, Monrovia, from Abidjan, in the Ivory Coast. This was all we needed to know. It was now possible to get into Liberia! We headed back to the UK immediately, and within a few weeks we were flying KLM to Abidjan, a bit nervous, not because of the possible dangers in Liberia but because we didn't know what to expect once we got to Abidjan. Tickets could not be bought in London for the last part of the journey, and with my poor French I was not looking forward to the transfer. I was soon to find there was good cause to be concerned.

CHAPTER 2

Abidjan to Monrovia

(October 20 & 21, 1991)

We arrived in Abidjan, commercial capital of the Ivory Coast, around mid-day on October 20, 1991. Everything was confusion and no one seemed eager to help us. Eventually we managed to find where to collect our luggage which consisted of two large suitcases; not much for a minimum stay of a whole year, but with the volatile conditions it was deemed best to travel light. The less we had the less we could loose.

After wandering around the main terminal looking for some sign that would suggest a flight to Monrovia, we were approached by a young man who offered his services to us. He did this in English so we accepted, though not without some misgivings. As he grabbed our trolley and went straight out of the main doors of the airport, it did pass through our minds that he might be about to steal them. However, it was a relief to discover that flights for West African destinations had their own booking hall and departure lounge. We trotted after him and he took us, and our luggage, to an annex of the main airport building. We were not unfamiliar with airports on the African continent, having served in Zimbabwe and Zambia, but here in the section of the airport reserved for short haul flights it was truly chaotic. Flight numbers and destinations were chalked badly onto a greasy black board and fifty or sixty people were very noisily milling around one small counter.

At first, I thought they all wanted to get to Liberia, but fortunately I was mistaken. The officials were speaking in French, much too fast for me to understand what they were saying, but we still needed to buy tickets for the last stage of our journey. We had no option but to rely on the young man who had brought us to this place of confusion, for we knew no one else. Fearing that he could run off with our cash and passports, we tried hard to keep him within our sight but he soon disappeared into the mass of bodies at the counter. All we could do was what we soon learned was the only option in many situations that we were to find ourselves - we prayed. To our great relief, he eventually returned to give us the news that the flight to Monrovia was almost full but we should hurry to have our luggage weighed. To our great surprise, when we got to the counter we were told to stand on the scales together with everything we had brought with us. Smiling a little with embarrassment we complied, but sadly, in spite the combined weight of Dorothy and I being less than 265 lbs and our cases being well within the 45 lbs limit, we were informed that the plane to Liberia could not take both of us, and our luggage, on the same flight. Either one of us would have to wait in Abidjan until the next flight in a few days time, or we would have to leave our luggage to follow on the flight later in the week.

Our experience in Africa had taught us never to be parted from our luggage and we certainly did not consider for one moment being separated from each other; so the plane left without us and our luggage. We sat, not sure of what to do or where to go.

We had no visa for the Ivory Coast, so technically, we could not leave the airport. We also learned that the plane that had just left without us was not returning for at least three days. Once again, however, it seems the Lord had been kind to us. We discovered that the young man who had helped us so far, was actually a Liberian, and enjoyed talking about Liberia. More importantly, he also informed us there was a hotel within the airport that we could use. Aware that we wanted to get to Liberia as soon as possible, he introduced us to his friend, a policeman, who, he said, could get one of us out of the airport, without the required visa, in order to purchase a ticket. This was especially useful because we had heard that the following day there would be an Air Guinea flight to Monrovia which, if we could get tickets, would suit us fine. We had been warned about visitors to some African countries getting taxi rides never to be seen again, or at the very least to be robbed and left by the roadside in the middle of nowhere. Nevertheless, I felt the risk had to be taken, so I let our young facilitator get a cab for me and asked him take me to a travel agency in town while Dorothy was left praying for my safe return in the hotel room. Thankfully I arrived back with the tickets about two hours later. Of course the young helper and policeman had cost us quite a few American dollars but we felt we had got off lightly; we had a bed for the night and a ticket for the flight in the morning. At the end of the day we thanked God for the remarkable way his prevenient grace had gone before us and provided all the help we needed. This was something we were to discover time and again as we lived and worked for the next 13 years in Liberia.

The next day we had our chocolate croissant and black tea, then found our own way to the terminal for local traffic. There we met Nabile Haider, a Lebanese business man, who for our first year in Liberia was a helpful associate until he returned to his family in Canada after a nasty experience with some of Taylor's rebel militia. Sitting waiting for the plane to arrive, he was able to point out to us the names of some of the people who were returning with us to Liberia. People like Father Hickey who had been deported during the Doe regime for speaking out against human right abuses was there, together with various other government officials from past regimes. The words of advice he gave us as we waited for the plane, which was already about three hours over due, were words of wisdom that came to mind frequently during our stay in Liberia; "*You must go with heaps of 'patience'*." Seeing how so many of the 'big' people of Liberia were returning it was clear at that time many people believed the Peace Keepers (ECOMOG) would either quash the civil war quickly, or that a negotiated peace would evolve without much more fighting now that President Doe had been killed. However, we were soon to discover that the then leader of the rebellion, Charles Taylor, had a very different agenda.

When we walked out onto the tarmac and boarded the Air Guinea plane, we found to our horror that it had been used mostly as a cargo plane for transporting local marketers with their produce around the surrounding country districts. There was no air-conditioning, the seats were torn and it was without any seatbelts, added to which, the chicken feathers which floated in the cabin were accompanied by a rather pungent smell. However, we were on the last leg of our journey to Liberia, having waited for 17 months, and now we just prayed that the one officer couple who were supposed to have met us the previous day would be at the airport when we arrived. We didn't have any idea where the apartment rented for us was located.

As we circled the airfield preparing to land, we were dismayed to see, not just helicopters and planes destroyed by fighting on the ground, but more particularly the two passenger planes that had clearly not made the landing safely. This was only a small airport with a short runway used in times of peace, solely for internal flights. The main international airport, large enough for the very biggest planes, was at this time in the hands of Charles Taylor's rebels. As we slowly drew to a halt just a few yards from the end of the runway there was a ripple of applause and we all alighted from the plane as quickly as possible.

Happily, in the small crowd waiting for passengers there was one couple clearly standing out from the rest with their white Salvation Army uniforms. Once again God had gone before us because on the previous day the lady who had gratefully accepted our seat on the plane had seen Lieutenant Ben Gaymo and recognized his uniform. So she passed on the news that we should be expected any time soon, as she had seen us in Abidjan. Little were we to know that it would be another thirteen years before we would say goodbye in earnest to the 'Glorious Land of Liberty', as Liberia is so called on her National Seal.

Neither were we aware of the many dangers, thrills and blessings that awaited us before we would finally depart from Liberia.

CHAPTER 3

Adapting to Life in Liberia

If the terminal at Abidjan had been chaotic then Spriggs Paine airport, where we had touched down, was that and a lot more besides. Apart from there being utter confusion, it was also frightening, not least because the first thing we were ordered to do was to drop our passports into a large wickerwork basket.

Before heading for Liberia we had tried to read background accounts of Liberia, including some relating to visitors' experiences. There were many stories of people, supposedly with faulty documents, being intimidated into paying large sums to avoid imprisonment. We wondered what the fate of someone without a passport would be at this time in Monrovia.

Now without passports, we were ushered into a tin hut with the other thirty or so other passengers. There were only a few Europeans, and we were left until last to be interviewed by a very serious looking official, guarded by two well armed but poorly dressed soldiers. On his desk were all the passengers' passports which were a relief to see. We had taken the trouble to get visas before we left England, and now hoped that there was nothing we had left undone. Though abrupt, the official was not rude and just asked questions. Some, like, "*why have you come to Liberia?*" were easy to answer but '*where are you going stay?*' presented us with a big problem; all we knew was that it was an apartment in a district known as Mamba Point.

At this stage of the interrogation we asked for Lieutenant Gaymo, who had initially been refused entry, to be allowed into the office to help us with the details. Reluctantly this was agreed, and the lieutenant did manage to assure the official that we were not rebel spies or arms dealers. It seems the man had met our predecessor, Major Millar, on one occasion so, our title of Captain did not create the misconception I had feared it could have in a country torn apart by several opposing armies. At least in Liberia the lingua franca was English, or should I say 'American'. I dreaded to think what this interview would have been like if the questioning had all been in French or Swahili!

The Customs hall, where our baggage had been taken, was a different shed, heavily guarded by ECOMG soldiers. Every item in our two cases and hand luggage was scrutinised and again we were glad we had travelled light. Once safely through the immigration and customs procedures we took a taxi to our quarters at Mamba Point, not very far from the American Embassy and opposite the International Red Cross building. Major Len Millar had kindly gone back into Monrovia for a couple of weeks before us in order to find somewhere for us to live, but he had returned to Canada by the time we arrived in Liberia. He had told us it was situated in the part of the city believed to be the safest. We didn't get that impression, when we looked at the building rented for our quarters, and saw how well peppered with bullet holes it was! Even inside the lounge a mirror had cracks radiating out from the point where it had been penetrated by a bullet of some kind without shattering. The quarters was a two bed-roomed furnished apartment formerly the home for a wealthy Liberian in more peaceful times but now it was showing the effects of almost two years of war. We soon discovered that 'safest' did not mean 'safe' for we had only been there for a matter of days when a small restaurant, two buildings away, was attacked during the night and blown up by a hand-grenade.

As we drove into the centre of Monrovia from the airport, we could hardly believe that we were in the capital city of any country. Nearly every building had been damaged to some degree and, as a consequence of the tropical climate, lush green plants were already growing out from the walls of the abandoned properties. We were surprised to see so few people on the streets, and a complete lack of animal life of any sort. We had been used to seeing dogs, cats and chickens in the streets and yards of African homes but, here there were none. Later we were informed that they had all been eaten.

Life had become extremely tough for the ordinary person while Monrovia was besieged by Charles Taylor's rebel forces. For several months aid agencies had found it very difficult to distribute any food to the city's population who had been close to starving.

When we arrived all the normal utility services in Monrovia had ceased to operate; no water, no electricity, no telephones and no garbage collection. Those who could afford it had stand-by generators but the one for our apartment had long since been looted. After a couple of months in the apartment men came round asking us if we would like to be connected to a power line for the supply of electricity. Unfortunately, the line was often disconnected and so during the ten months we were in this building we had long periods without electricity which mostly affected our cooking requirements, not to mention the lack of any air conditioner or fans. Candles and early nights became normal, even though in England I seldom went to bed before midnight. Now it was an hour or so with candles and then to bed at eight o'clock, though not necessarily to sleep because it was so hot and humid.

For cooking, Dorothy had no choice but to turn to the Liberian method which was to use a 'coal pot' burning charcoal. It was very primitive; just a bowl for the charcoal to burn on and a space beneath it for the ash to drop into. The saucepan or kettle had to be rested on top of the coals. After about six months we found a calor-gas cooker which worked well until supplies of gas ran out. Later we were to learn that the helpful engineers who had been connecting and reconnecting our power line were not officials of the electricity board, but former workers who were hooking us up to the executive line; a facility which was just supposed to serve the acting president and the executive buildings.

Major Millar had hired a helper for us before he had left and his main job was to guard the house when we were out and to fetch water from a well in the grounds of a school just two hundred metres away. However, water became a greater problem when, after a couple of months, displaced people were housed in the school and access to the well was denied. For a few months this meant a taxi ride for our helper, simply to get water from another well. Collecting water from the roof and using all water very sparingly became a real necessity.

Getting rid of rubbish was also a problem for there was no dustmen. We waited for some one to come begging and then we would do a deal; we would give him something if he would take away our trash. There were a few sites, mostly the gardens of bombed out buildings, where rubbish was left for collection, roughly once a month. Often it spilled onto the road before anything was done to remove it, with no regard being given to the obnoxious smells that wafted from it or any associated health hazards.

During that first year, while we were still living at Mamba Point, we had some interesting visitors like the Bishop, clothed in very tatty vestments. He kept calling to beg for money and even asking us to take over his churches. He said he had three but we never went to see them as it was clear he still wanted to keep control over them and we were sure it would mean trouble once the Army began to appoint their leaders.

This had been the sad experience at several of the little churches that were first incorporated into The Salvation Army in Liberia. Often they were being run by the person who had founded them so when the Army began to appoint new leaders the former leaders sometimes walked off with half of its members.

One of the first things that we had noticed as we drove into the capital from the airport, and also when we were eventually able to move around outside of Monrovia, was the multitude of church signs. It appeared superficially that Liberia was a very religious country, but it was not long before we discovered that in this country running a church was called doing 'God business' as many of the churches were being run for the financial benefit of their leaders and not with any great spiritual purpose. Some of these were quite large and well attended, with various practices that were clearly syncretistic mixes of Christianity and various forms of animism. Some of the largest expressions of such churches were also very 'prosperity-centred' with congregations being invited to pay money for miracles that would bring financial gain or some other benefit to them or members of their family. Often payments would be graduated, depending on the likely gain to be answered by a prayer. It was not uncommon for prayers to be offered for God to find a wealthy husband or wife, a good job or a visa for the USA. These practices were some times even seen enacted on the streets of Monrovia. It was noticeable that Nigerians were often the leaders of the churches selling 'blessings'.

There were of course, most of the mainstream churches (see Appendix i) who were the mainstay of the education and health systems, both in the towns and the interior.

Our neighbour was an Indian man who, we later discovered, was on the run from the police in Europe. In the apartment above him there was a Liberian family. The husband had been the manager of a bank that had gone into liquidation. This was quite a common event in Liberia, where some unscrupulous business people would open a bank and use its capital for theirs and their friend's personal unsecured loans. The banking system was clearly in a mess as I found out when I wanted to cash some travellers' checks. No one wanted to touch them because the international banking system did not trust them and so normal activities were not being carried out. However, there was one trust bank, run by Americans and which was used to pay aid workers and those working for American subsidiaries. Even they charged me ten percent to cash them.

Our Liberian neighbour, however, was very friendly and invited us up for tea one day to show us a video. He told us it was about the previous president, Master Sergeant Samuel K. Doe. We felt this was a good opportunity to get to know our neighbour, and so politely accepted his offer. We were soon to wish we hadn't.

The video began with the overthrow of the previous government and the killing of President Tolbert. To our horror, it showed the parading of most of the ministers of the previous regime, being taken naked from prison to the beach. They were then tied to poles and executed by a firing squad. But worse was to follow. It then went on to show how President Doe himself was captured by one of the rebel leaders, Prince Johnson. It horrifically showed Doe being mutilated, starting with the cutting off of both his ears, in an effort to get him to tell them where he had hidden the millions of dollars he was believed to have had hidden away. While we had to turn away, our neighbour and his son were chuckling and even loudly laughing. It was then that we realised we had come to a country where cruelty and death were viewed in a very different way to us and where the message of Jesus was still badly needed, in spite of the prolific number of churches.

Mamba Point had been an affluent district of Monrovia before the war, so the Bishop was not the only caller we had seeking financial help or a job. Several of our present youthful Salvationist, were saved after we had just arrived from the UK with no material things I could give them. However, I did invite them to come into our quarters if they would like to know more about us and what our mission was all about.

This led to our spare room becoming a veritable mercy seat. As they learned something about the Salvation Army and about us, including our reasons for coming to such a dangerous place, we had the joy of seeing several life-changing decisions being made. Most of those who accepted Christ then are now active Salvationists living, the life of born again Christians.

Just up the hill from us was a grand building with ornate gates. If we had come two years before it would have been a place we would have taken pride in, for it was the British Embassy building. However, in the very early days of the civil war the embassy had closed completely and when we arrived it was in the hands of the Americans. It had now become an annex of the American Embassy.

Clearly, no help in an emergency could be expected to come from the British Diplomatic Corps; in fact the British Foreign Office was simply telling everyone not to go to Liberia. However, we registered our names with the American Embassy and the following day wrote to ask for an interview with the ambassador, his Excellency Peter de Voss. We had been in the country for a few weeks and wanted to see if he had any advice to pass on to us.

During our audience he was able to give us some valuable information about the history of the country, both distant and recent. He also gave us some advice for our personal safety, though I have to admit, we did not always follow it. Along with his advice he presented us with a very informative book on Liberia, sadly lost when we were looted in 1996, that gave us insights to the traditions of the native Liberian. It also gave some very graphic illustrations of the activities of the once very powerful Society of Masons whose grand marble temple was not far from the American Embassy. However, the ambassador was a Christian and I knew he understood that we were the representatives of a Christian church. He told us that in the USA he had met The Salvation Army many times in the course of his work. So, before we left his office, I asked him where he thought would be the best place for us to begin our mission and what we should concentrate on. He believed the best course of action was for us to seek to win over the youth of the nation for, though they might seem at present to be the destroyers of the country, in the future the building of the new nation would be largely their responsibility. This coincided exactly with our thoughts, and we took it as God's endorsement of the course of action we had already begun.

Another aspect of living in Monrovia at this time that made us feel vulnerable was the lack of communication with people inside as well as outside of the country. We had no phone or fax. In fact there were very few telephones still working in the country, and if emails had been invented we certainly did not know anything about them. To make a call it was necessary to go to the telephone exchange and pay US dollars in advance for the length of call that was to be made. However, the queue was always just a mass of people as it seemed that everyone in Monrovia wanted to make calls to the States and that their relatives all wanted to share the same phone. To save spending time behind a long queue we opted to make our calls to our family and our headquarters in the UK after dark. It was really a bit of a risk, because there were often explosions and shooting during the evening time as Monrovia was a lawless place. No police were ever seen on the streets after dark. The lack of electricity also meant that there were no street or shop lights. It was pitch black with only lots of flickering candles along the road side as petty traders still tried to sell tiny items. Without street lights the many broken paving slabs and the open storm drains also became a serious hazard. The one consolation was that it was a bit cooler at night and, even though there was still a small queue, the waiting was not so painful. Few Westerners would walk out at night but I saw little alternative.

One other vital factor on the communications front was that we had no vehicle. The Salvation Army's jeep had been looted during the attack on the city in 1990, and naturally enough International Headquarters were not prepared to arrange for another to be sent until there was a good likelihood of some stability, at least in Monrovia. We were therefore faced with either walking or using a taxi. Both alternatives had things for and against them. Dorothy and I both liked walking, and saw it as one way of keeping fit and meeting people, but with the lunchtime temperature in the shade averaging around 100° F, walking was exhausting. It was six months before we took delivery of our new Land Rover. Taxis should have been more attractive than walking in the searing heat but in Liberia these were like nothing we could have imagined.

The war had taken its toll with all forms of transport in the country. Buses, which had once been numerous, were now left lifeless by the wayside. Gradually they were being turned into skeletons as the makers of coal pots chiselled and cut their way through the panelling. The windows had long been extracted to be used for squatter housing. Many taxis were suffering the same fate, while others were cannibalised to enable some to be drivable. Of those on the road some had no windscreens, or had almost as much masking tape as window. Others had little or no foam on the seats, which became increasingly uncomfortable when four or even five people were squeezed on the back seat and two on the front. Often doors had to be held closed by the passengers and on one occasion I found myself sitting in the front seat with the petrol tank between my legs. The real tank had been replaced by a polythene container and hitched up to the carburettor through the front dashboard. I just told myself that if we did have a crash the 'end' would be swift.

Gradually we developed the routine of using a taxi on Sundays when we would be carrying thirty song books (the only surviving items from the time of Major Millar) and walking most other times during the week.

On one occasion we were made to think a little more seriously about using the taxis when Mrs. Gaymo helped Dorothy catch a taxi after a mid-week women's meeting. She hailed the taxi and then, before letting the driver drive off, she told him she had taken his number and would know how to trace him if Dorothy did not reach her destination safely. As they drove off Dorothy found the driver to be very a sincere Muslim, who was unlikely to harm a fly.

In fact he was concerned about our safety, for he had seen a crowd around us on the Saturday and had thought we might have been in trouble. What he had seen was simply a peaceful open-air service, but he was not to know that. The longer we stayed in Liberia, however, the more we learned why Mrs. Gaymo had lectured the driver like she had. Abductions and mutilations were not uncommon, particularly at election times.

During the first two or three weeks we were given various sightings of the original jeep but they all proved to be hoaxes to elicit money from us. Fortunately very little was lost because we always offered to recompense the finder once we were shown the vehicle or it was brought to us. To our great relief, in April, 1992, the new jeep did arrive, thanks to the generosity of The Salvation Army in Canada,

Knowing that the official language in Liberia was English, we assumed we would have no trouble with understanding and conversing with people. However, to start with the language was English as from the USA, so we did not have pavements we had 'sidewalks' and petrol was 'gas', diesel was 'fuel oil' and taps were 'faucets' and so on. This was not too bad for us because films and T.V. had spread such deviations across most of the world but we had not expected the special Monrovia accent which at first was like a foreign language to us.

I can now understand the problem people have when they visit England from abroad and are met by people with broad Scot's, Geordie, or Cockney accents. In Zimbabwe we experienced no trouble at all understanding the English spoken in the cities or in country regions but in Liberia it took a long time before we really understood what most people were saying. I expect Liberians probably got quite bored with us having to get them to repeat what they were saying several times before we understood them. Listening carefully, we came to realize that they were missing the final letter from the ends of many words and they even abbreviated sentences, so a lot was left to guess work. For instance; a reply to the question about when something had taken place would be "Ever since". Not only was it difficult for us to understand Monrovians but it was just as difficult for many of them to understand us.

Our efforts to be clear and precise with our pronunciation often made matters worse rather than better, because the urban Liberians were familiar with a very different intonation. These problems occasionally led to some big mistakes being made through misinterpretations. The strange thing was, those who had been taught English in rural country schools were understood better by us and, I think, understood us more easily, than the town people. There were more than a dozen indigenous languages in Liberia, some of them totally unrelated to each other. It was therefore not possible for us to learn more than a few odd greetings as it could have been seen that we were favouring one tribe more than another. Like almost everywhere in Africa, a degree of sensitivity had to be exercised when dealing with things that were tribal in nature.

CHAPTER 4

First Impressions of Our Church

Three days after getting off the plane we went for our 'Welcome meeting', in the only one of our churches that was still functioning in Monrovia.

Lieutenant Gaymo collected us from the apartment and had a taxi waiting for us. It was one of the better ones, though it had no back window. When it dropped us off we had to go down a very rough path to what was clearly the start of a squatter area. When we saw the church it was not a complete shock to us, Major Millar had shown us photographs of it, but it was not a pretty sight. The church building was only partly finished and the entrance was through a rusty tin hut that had formerly been the main church.

It was in a corner of a district called Sinkor which before the civil war was mostly for the wealthy Liberians and contained the majority of foreign embassies. However, the church was in a part that had been reclaimed years before from the coastal swamps and which was now occupied by squatters. Once through the entrance we found the church was not as bad as we thought for it was a proper cement block building with a zinc roof and hardboard ceiling.

We were greeted by a congregation of fifteen adults: the two officers, three men and ten ladies, plus four or five children. Having been told that nearly everyone in Monrovia spoke English, we were surprised to discover that this congregation were mostly people who could understand very little English. They were mostly uneducated people who only spoke their own tribal language, Bassa. Initially it was clear that these people were happy that we had come, but a little later we discovered that really we were a big disappointment to most of them for they had expected us to come 'bearing gifts'. This was understandable for they were very poor and their needs were great, but we came carrying just a bare minimum of essential things, not cases full of relief supplies.

Starting with nothing but the Gospel to give out actually helped us to centre our thoughts and activities round our primary mission, to convert the unsaved. We knew that sooner or later the work would include relief to the starving, medicine to the sick and education for those needing schooling, but that was to be in the future; they would all need to include a strong commitment to evangelism.

Initially, we wanted to establish The Salvation Army as a Church, distinct from the numerous international relief agencies that were already established.

After three weeks attending the Sunday worship service at Sinkor it became clear that there was no requirement for two pair of officers at the Corps, so we decided to look for Salvationists on the other side of the town, in a district know as Bushrod Island. The port was in this part of the city and it used to contain some light industries, though there was very little activity when we arrived.

Before the war there had been a small Salvation Army corps which held its services in the Boatswain High School. We had been informed that in 1989, when Lieutenant Barr, a Ghanaian officer, had been appointed as its leader some members had broken away because of their loyalties toward its former leader, who had also been its founder. We were to discover that such schisms had happened in several other Corps outside of Monrovia.

This was not, however, the main reason for Bushrod Island's complete demise. Its members had been almost exclusively Nigerian and Ghanaian and when the ECOMOG peacekeeping troops, who were also mostly Nigerian and Ghanaian, arrived in the capital and prevented the rebel leader Charles Taylor capturing the city, he had threatened to kill any Nigerians or Ghanaians he found. The majority of these nationalities therefore sailed back to their homelands on the same ships that had brought the troops.

We advertised over the radio and in the newspaper that we were to reopen the Bushrod Island Salvation Army church on the third Sunday in November 1991. On the Saturday before this we held an open-air service in the fish market at the end of Jamaica Road, a hundred or so metres from where the school in which the corps had formerly met. That we looked a most unusual sight on the streets of Monrovia there was no doubt. Troop-carrying trucks stopped to see who we were and what we were doing, and we could hear people saying we were pilots, sea captains and even American marines (Dorothy found that very amusing seeing she was fifty-eight years old and just five feet two inches tall).

That, more than ever, brought home to us the fact that almost nobody in Liberia at that time knew anything about The Salvation Army. In more peaceful times when the wealthier and more travelled Liberians were around, we may have found it a little different, I suppose, but at that time we were looked upon by many as a strange sect with our 'S's on our shirts and a ministry without the sacraments of Baptism and the Eucharist. We were happy to know though that there was complete freedom of worship in Liberia and at that time there were no problems between the majority Christian and the large minority Muslim population.

The result of that first open-air service was a congregation the following day of three men and three boys, with a tiny little girl tightly holding a brother's hand. Some may have thought this was a failure, but God knew differently. From that group one of the men became an officer and two of the children eventually became senior soldiers, one of whom was a very successful command mission team leader.

We had been surprised that no previous members had shown up on that first Sunday service, but some weeks later, Elijah Sowen, a former junior solder, did come back and is now an active Salvationist at the City Corps. With the help of The Salvation Army, Elijah has become a fully qualified teacher with a BA degree. At the time of writing he is working in the Army's educational secretariat.

Another former member, a Ghanaian called Afari Minta, also returned to the corps with a story of a miraculous escape from rebel soldiers. He had travelled into the interior just prior to Taylor turning against all Ghanaians and was with his daughter in the Bomi Hills District, where rebels were rounding up all Ghanaians and Nigerians. They were in hiding for some weeks but his daughter got very sick. He decided to try to carry her to a clinic but, as he feared, was spotted by one of the rebels. However, his past good life was on his side. The rebel recognized him as his former mathematics teacher and greeted him as a friend. He even found a wheelbarrow and helped him get the girl to a clinic several miles' walk away. Both he and the girl survived and eventually they arrived back in Monrovia.

Of course there was much more to the story but Afari says he had one chorus kept passing through his head during his ordeal which was; "*I know the Lord will make a way for me*" – and He did!

Afari eventually went back to Ghana with his family and became an envoy.

In spite of the problems with transport we steadily built up the little group at Bushrod Island by continuing with our Saturday open-airs, Sunday services, Bible studies and sick visitation. We even added a Sunday morning march from the fish market, until the torrential rains arrived in late April.

One of the signs that people were getting well saved was the way they were putting their lives in order. The owner of the house on whose veranda we used to hold our Bible Studies came to me one day to say that he was impressed with what we were doing because, since William (one of his lodgers, who eventually became an officer) had 'got religion' at the Salvation Army, ladies were no longer going in and out of his room!

After about nine months we enrolled our first soldiers, junior and senior.

One of the problems was, however, to find uniforms. As second-hand navy blue trousers and skirts were obtainable from clothing markets, we chose to use these as our uniform. Even obtaining these was a problem for some. Another problem was obtaining blue epaulettes and junior soldiers' badges. To start with, Dorothy bought some blue material and hand-stitched the epaulettes. Silver S's were put on them from some spare officer's trimmings we had brought with us. The junior soldiers were given a blue patch with a silver 'S' on it.

Try as we might, we could never find any tailor who could sew a good 'S' onto the epaulettes but eventually we found one of our hostel boys who could sew the epaulettes and a young man in town who could print S's on them using a silk screen method. This is the method still used in Liberia. As time went by, we had friends and corps all over England, including Dunstable, Tunbridge Wells, Sutton, Reading, Cambridge, Stowmarket, Norwich and many more, collecting white shirts/blouses and navy trousers/skirts for us. These were sent out in containers which brought us vital items like generators which in our early years were unobtainable in Liberia.

We held the first wedding in our quarters when Anthony Sio, and Munah, his partner at that time, got converted and wanted to have a marriage blessing. So the happy couple made their vows to each other in our lounge. They later became officers, and at the time of writing are divisional officers in charge of Bassa District.

With the steady growth of the Bushrod Island Corps, we followed up on work that had already been done by our predecessors, Majors Dorothy and Leonard Millar, and managed to purchase the one lot of land (a quarter of an acre) already earmarked by them. Building started in September 1993 and was completed by April of the following year.

Sadly Lieutenant Matthew Dogbah, who had taken over the corps in July, 1992, following training in Ghana, fled the country for the USA in December 1993, leaving his wife to struggle on with the corps and children. This soon proved too much for her but the corps had been firmly rooted and is now a fully functioning Salvation Army corps.

Bushrod Island Corps has never grown as large as some this partly due to many of its members having moved to the other side of town. One reason for this was because they wanted to attend or teach at one of the Army's schools. Others found employment at our new Command Headquarters and some, I am happy to say, left to become officers.

CHAPTER 5

The Salvation Army School System

We hadn't been long in Liberia before Lieutenant Gaymo began to make some rather pointed observations about how all true churches in Liberia had their own schools. He pointed out that there had been a small Salvation Army school held in Buchanan Church before the war that no longer existed.

After putting it to God in prayer, I decided it would be good for evangelism and helpful for public awareness if we could open a school in Monrovia. So the search for suitable property in which to house a school began. As I had been a schoolmaster for fourteen years in the UK and had also been in charge of a boarding school in Zimbabwe at the start of our missionary service, I did have the right credentials. Nevertheless, it was still an enormous challenge.

The state of school buildings in Monrovia was terrible but it was the capital city and prior to the war schools were generally of a respectable standard. Some very substandard schools had sprung up because of the war but I knew the Army had a high reputation throughout the world for its schools and we had to do our best. There were other challenges too; the education system in Liberia was based on the American one, not the UK's and, with so much destruction all around, it was going to be hard to find somewhere suitable to house a school.

Len Millar School

Eventually the lieutenant found a building with seven small rooms. It was not ideal, it was dark with no proper windows, and extremely hot, because of its low roof, but it became our first Len Millar School. It was called the Len Millar School in honour of our predecessor who had been the first leader of The Salvation Army in Liberia.

We painted it and repaired the roof as best we could and opened it as an elementary school two blocks down 17th Street, from the Tubman Boulevard. When inspected by an official from the ministry of education, we were told that the teaching was up to standard but the accommodation was not what was expected of The Salvation Army. I knew this was because she had seen The Salvation Army at work in the States. I didn't think this was a very fair comparison, but we too could see that it was far from ideal. We continued to look for better premises. Eventually one of our new soldiers introduced me to the head of the Barnes family who owned the three-storied building that formerly housed the Ministry of Youth and Sport. This was right on the main road into the centre of the city, very visible, giving The Salvation Army the high profile I had been seeking.

I believed it needed to be visible, and this became a major consideration in the coming years when we were looking for land on which to build our churches and schools.

After the usual bargaining session necessary in Africa before any deal is clinched, we sealed an agreement for a ten-year lease of the property, and spent a lot of money repairing the building. Some mocked us, saying it would all be destroyed by rockets or mortars, because just as we began work, Charles Taylor's rebel forces attacked the city with campaign 'Octopus'; advancing on the city from all sides.

We were convinced God wanted His work to go forward and that this school was an important step in the progress of our church's ministry. So, unlike some expatriates, we stayed and pressed on with the work. When the building was ready it was possible to house almost 600 students from ABC to Grade 10.

A few weeks before we opened the building as a school, we brought members from both the Sinkor Corps and the newly formed Bushrod Island Corps together for a march of witness from the market to the school and there commenced what was soon to be known as the Monrovia City Corps.

This new building was soon found to be too small to house everyone who wanted to attend the school but within a year we were also able to lease another building just a hundred metres away. That then became the Senior High School with just over 200 students for Grades 10, 11 and 12. The first principal of the new school was Mr. Taweh Johnson, M.Sc. He was, at that time, the senior Mathematics lecturer at the Liberia University, which was not then functioning as a university. He later went on to be the School Education System's Technical Advisor for The Salvation Army in Liberia, as well as a faithful and loyal soldier of the City corps.

I soon discovered that there were many added complications to running schools in a war situation, particularly when the government was made up from various warring factions. From the start we worked on the basis that the fees paid by the students must cover the costs of the day-to-day expenses of running the school including the costs of the teachers' salaries. Though in more peaceful times the government had helped by providing salaries for some teachers, there were no longer any grants of this kind. The fact was that roles were reversed and various government departments worked hard, with a degree of intimidation, to extract whatever they could from us for the privilege of operating a school!

The problem was, we were not sure what was legal and what was not when it came to the demands of visiting officials. When they arrived in a group of six demanding money for various reasons it was very intimidating as they were always sent to me. I seldom agreed that we owed the authorities anything but simply gave them an allowance for their taxi ride back to their offices. After some years, when we had progressed to having a retained counsellor (solicitor) and a smart young man, Lawson Warbey, as our accountant, they were less worry to me. In the first instance they would be directed to Lawson and I would make myself unavailable. He would keep them waiting for an hour or so and never offer anything to help transport them back. Gradually their visits became less frequent. When they really got nasty, as they could, I simply sent for our counsellor who was well able to sort right from wrong and truth from the falsehood. Even in the rural areas we had some of these problems when we started to move out of the city with our school work.

As I have mentioned, the Liberia education system was modelled on the USA's, and this included the morning ritual of raising the flag and singing the National Anthem while saluting the flag. During this procedure every one stood still. I understood that but, what I didn't know was that whenever the flag is lowered at 6 p.m. a whistle is blown and you are expected to stand still wherever you are. This was also carried out at all government establishments; if you were anywhere near when the whistle sounds, you must stop! On one occasion I was spoken to very seriously by a policeman, when in my ignorance I did not halt when the whistle was sounded for the flag to be lowered outside of a police station.

We did have a nasty incident concerning the flagpole at the Len Millar School when, trying to be helpful, a nine year old boy climbed up the flagpole when he saw the rope had hitched and needed pulling down. Having successfully accomplished what he had gone to do, he then slid down the pole, forgetting the attachment around which the rope was tied at the foot of the pole. The boy came down fast and ripped a huge lump of flesh out of the inside of his thigh. Fortunately I was standing near by and, he was quickly placed in my jeep and, with a teacher at his side, rushed him to the government hospital. Once there he was placed on a bed as nurses scurried away to find something with which to treat the wound; possibly an anti-tetanus injection and some bandages. To my utter amazement they could find nothing! They didn't even have any antiseptic with which to wash the wound.

I didn't hesitate; I picked him up, put him in the jeep again and rushed him to the Catholic hospital (I have to admit the cost factor had initially made me try the government hospital first). There they soon gave him the right treatment because I assured them that The Salvation Army would pay. To my joy and relief the boy was back at school, fully recovered, by the next semester. This really brought home to me the state of the government hospital at that time.

I was very pleased to find that our city schools, after their first year of operation, always generated enough funds from student fees to cover the day-to-day costs. One of the problems was to keep the balance between the fees charged to the students and the salaries paid to the teachers. On one occasion after the teachers had signed their annual contracts, several of them threatened not to mark any test papers or to teach unless they were given an increment to their salaries. I explained that the balance between fees and salaries was vital, so incremental increases could only be granted at a time when fees could also be increased, at the commencement of a new academic year. We held parents' meetings to discuss the matter and even got as far as promising an increment for the next year but at the end of the first semester they refused even to set the end of term's examinations. They were not only intimidating the management (me) but also the students because in the US education system exams are keys to academic progress.

Things got so bad that I dismissed six of the Len Millar High School staff and paid them the five month's salary as per their contracts. However, they continued to put pressure on the students and encouraged them to riot which caused a small amount of damage. The worst aspect was that the staff made it all very political because they belonged to the political faction that was, at that time, in charge of the Ministry of Education.

Intimidation then came from the ministry's office for us to reinstate them but by then the teachers had accepted the cash to close their contracts, so if they had returned they would have been working without getting paid for the next five months. I had to go to the Ministry of Education along with our counsellor and one or two supporters to reason with the Minister of Education.

Things got really nasty when the minister said over the national radio station that if the teachers were not reinstated he was going to close down the entire work of The Salvation Army in Liberia. I doubted whether he had the power to do such a thing but he could certainly make things very difficult to operate a school. This would have been doubly damaging to us as we were just about to start building another large school.

Fortunately, within days the minister went on a trip to the States and the deputy minister was much more understanding of our position. The rebellious teachers now had no support and two weeks later the Acting Minister of Education, along with the Minister for Youth and Sport, took part in the groundbreaking ceremony of the William Booth School. Both spoke and highly praised the work The Salvation Army was doing in Liberia.

This trouble was a disappointing episode in the history of our schools, made more hurtful because it followed shortly after the teachers had been given help in cash and rice as soon as I returned after the 1996 fighting in Monrovia; something that no other employer was prepared to do. It is also true that we prided ourselves that we always paid our staff on time every month, unlike many schools where the salaries were often months late and sometimes never came.

Some schools even contracted teachers just for ten or eleven months, leaving their families to struggle on for the extra month or two while schools were on the end of academic year vacation. Worse still, government teachers sometimes worked for years without receiving any salary. This led them to get involved in corruption, by accepting bribes (or demanding them) from students for giving unearned pass marks in the school tests without which they could not be promoted to the next grade. Sadly this produced a culture which was replicated in most branches of government, for the same reason, and did not disappear even when salaries were received regularly and on time, as in our schools.

Even at the time of writing bribery and corruption in nearly all schools is a big problem. It is almost impossible to eradicate because many staff and students find it convenient, while the honest ones don't like to expose the culprits and get their peers thrown out of a job or expelled from school.

It was never our policy to lease buildings if it could be avoided and though we had taken out a ten year lease on the Barnes building we were still looking for land on which to build our own Len Millar School. Eventually our good friend, Tony Hage, assisted us by putting us in touch with the owner, Mrs. Antoinette Tubman, of part of the former GSA land. There were some problems because one other Liberian family thought the land belonged to them, but after extensive research it was agreed by both parties that the portion of land we wanted to purchase was indeed the property of Mrs. Tubman. She was the widow of the most famous Liberian President.

We were thrilled to be able to buy this land as it was on the Boulevard that went right through the centre of town, on the route that every one would have to drive when travelling to and from the international airport. As it was only one acre and contained some buildings that we did not wish to destroy, we decided to build the High School with ground, first and second floors, and the Elementary School at the rear with just a ground and first floor. The two warehouses in between were eventually adapted to be a gymnasium (with changing rooms and basketball court) and a Chapel. We even managed to get a typing and computer school by adapting three smaller rooms. The bulk of the money for this, new Len Millar School, came from NORAD, a partnership between the government of Norway and The Salvation Army in that country.

Before construction work commenced in 2000, two big obstacles had to be overcome by the property manager/builder David Bainda; a huge Cotton tree had to be brought down and sawn up into planks, and two fuel tanks had to be dug up and removed from the site. Once this was achieved the sandy ground had to be compacted using a heavy roller, following which the footings could then be started. Without using any support machinery and relying solely on timber scaffolding, each phase of the project took a little over a year to complete and both were fully operational by September 2003.

The new Len Millar High School was equipped with ten administrative rooms, twenty-four classrooms, two wells and a fine library plus a laboratory which, though poorly equipped by Western standards, was one of the best school laboratories in the country at that time. The school was immediately very popular and I soon found that our rule that no class should contain more than 49 students was being broken by the registrars. Some classes did stay at 61 for the first year but a more reasonable level was arrived at for subsequent years. Once fully operational, it had a registration of over 1,300 students from ABC up to Grade 12.

William Booth School

Though the Len Millar School was the Army's first school to be started in Monrovia, it was not the first to have a purpose built building. Early in 1996 the Region was visited by two Canadian Officers, a representative from SAWSO and Major Inger Merit Nygård, the Projects officer and NORAD representative from Norway. This was the beginning of a great friendship between

Norway and Liberia as well as between my wife and myself with Major Inger Merit Nygård.

Our first meeting led to a partnership which was to be extremely productive over the following eight years in Liberia. The major brought vision, hope and valuable teaching skills on the drawing up of project proposals. Immediately following this meeting I drew up plans and proposals for a school to be built in three phases: Senior High School, Junior High School and Elementary School. In spite of the 1996 attack on the capital, when eventually we had to be air-lifted out of the country, the proposals were accepted and as soon as we got back into the Monrovia we began the search for a suitable site.

As with the Len Millar School it was Tony Hage's contacts with the former president's wife, Mrs. Antoinette Tubman, that provided us with land behind the Paynesville market. This site had formerly housed stables with a club house, and because we were going to use the land for a school and a church (school auditorium/ Paynesville Corps) Mrs. Tubman agreed to sell it to us. Tony informed us that it was also because of the respect she had for The Salvation Army that she had agreed to the sale. This was important because such people did not usually sell their land just for financial gain. The site was a large open field, big enough for all three schools to be built as single storeys, still leaving room for a large church building. There was even a spacious sports field and yet more room for expansion in the future. The church and high school went up very quickly as there were few complications.

By the end of the year 1997, the High School opened with 150 students. Within a year the Junior High was added, increasing its numbers to 800.

Now, with the further addition of the Elementary Department, it has more 1,300 students. For one year it did rise to almost 1,450 due to the pressure of parents to get their children into the school. By 2004 I believe this school must have been the most popular in the whole of Liberia because of its beautiful setting and for it high standard of teaching, exemplified that year by coming third in the National Examinations, when the top two were both full-time boarding schools. Every year we could have filled the school many times over.

In 2003 the size of the campus was doubled with the purchase of the rest of the land formerly owned by Mrs. Tubman. This is used as the football pitch at present but is large enough to include a 400 metres athletics running track (a future dream). When a cafeteria replaced the need for a kitchen it was converted into two classrooms and an office, which became the home of the William Booth Typing and Computer Institute. Later constructions on the campus included: a quarters for the Paynesville Corps officer, a dormitory for thirty boys' and a clinic. When we left Liberia in 2004, this campus had, for six years, been the venue for our Command Congresses (the gathering together of Salvationists from all over the country) but we were having to consider, with attendances topping the six-hundred mark, ways to cover the full size basketball court in front of the High School, in order to accommodate everyone.

Everywhere we went we were being asked by people, including government ministers and Senate Representatives, to bring the Army to their home districts. Though we would have loved to have believed it was the church they wanted, we knew it was mostly for our schools. We had to be very careful not to make promises that we could not keep.

School Bus Incident

There he was; the driver of the School bus was lying dead at the entrance to the security gate with his head cracked open, and his brains along side him. It was a horrific sight, the like of which my wife and I had never seen. The young security guard for our compound was still whimpering. He had come up the back stairs to our apartment screaming; '*He's dead, he's dead.*'

We had heard the banging on the steel gate at the entrance to our yard and the horn belonging to the school bus, but that was simply for the security lad to open the gate so the bus could be driven into the yard where it was always kept for the night. The guard was slow to respond to the horn, so the driver had alighted from the cab in order to go through the pedestrian entrance to pull the bolt and open the double gate himself. Foolishly, he had left the engine running and the handbrake off.

As he approached the pedestrian gate, the bus caught up with him. His head was compacted onto the concrete gate pillar, and in a split second his head was cracked open. He died instantly and his brains were emptied on the step beside him.

The security lad kept making a pathetic moaning and groaning sound. I don't know if it was shock that he was suffering from or a guilty conscience. If he had done his job properly the bus driver would not have got out of his cab to be hit by the bus.

Once we had got over the dreadful shock of this tragedy I had to move fast. A crowd was gathering and soon there were likely to be accusations flying around that might reflect on me and The Salvation Army. Some policemen arrived out of nowhere and they seemed more interested in me than the dead man and his possible relatives. I then thought to ring up Tony Hage. In situations like this, he was the best person to whom I could turn. As usual he was quick to assess the situation, and phoned up a police colonel with whom he was on good terms. To my great relief the police colonel arrived within a few minutes. He quickly took charge of the case, and I felt greatly assured. To get more money out of me and The Salvation Army, the police who arrived first could have placed blame upon me and arrested me. It was clearly not the colonel's intention to do that.

He made arrangements for the body to be taken to a funeral parlour, and I sent word for the driver's son to come to me. He was a registrar at the William Booth Elementary School. The Salvation Army paid for all the funeral expenses and because he was actually a non-active AFL soldier he was given a military funeral. After some serious and lengthy discussions, his wife was given US$1,000 and a child of his was given a scholarship at the Len Millar School. Our sympathy went out to the driver's family and I believe our support (financial and caring) was appreciated by them. The police colonel had to be paid as well, of course, but he was not greedy (perhaps Tont Hage had rewarded him as well). We were fortunate to get off so lightly.

The bus officially seated seventy-one passengers and formerly had been a school bus in the United States. These busses had been quite common in Liberia before the war but they were now lying around various fields where they were steadily being cut up to make 'coal pots' and various items for domestic and agricultural use.

It was Colonel Norris who helped us import our bus. We told him how much he could spend on our behalf and he scoured the bus garages in Chicago looking for a bargain. He found a suitable vehicle and then, with his wife, drove it all the way to Baltimore with his own car being towed at the rear. This was a true act of kindness from one of our past leaders, who we now consider to be our great friend. I believe it must have cost much more than we were charged, and our thanks go to the Central Territory of The Salvation Army in the United States of America.

The Salvation Army School System was, at this time, the first to get such a vehicle back on the roads for the benefit of its students. It was something that gave every student, in fact all Salvationists, a sense of pride in the whole organization. Having the bus enabled us to go as far as Gbarnga with school teams to compete in basketball and soccer with girls' teams as well as boys'. It was there that Dorothy had her first taste of watching basketball and came away saying she had thoroughly enjoyed the experience. On another occasion the band went there to take part in a marching parade, using our yellow bus to transport them.

Unfortunately the state of the roads and the high salt content of the air in Monrovia took its toll on the state of the bus's roadworthiness. The engine was fine but parts like the brakes became a constant worry. The now deceased driver had been the one to spot the needs of the bus and to initiate its repair. This had meant searching all the places where similar buses, operating before the fighting, had been left to be cannibalized. The new younger driver was good but was not very knowledgeable when it came to replacing parts for which a search was necessary. So eventually the bus was parked in the yard of the Girls' Hostel awaiting its own cannibalisation.

It had served the schools and The Salvation Army well for the time it was on the road. It had been the first of the big long yellow buses to appear on the roads since the out break of the war in Monrovia. It had helped many children to get to their schools, and this was not restricted to Salvation Army schools. With the words 'The Salvation Army School System' and the red shield logo emblazoned boldly on each side of the bus, it had given The Salvation Army in general and our school system in particular a high profile. This didn't only boost our standing in Monrovia, for as we went further afield we found the good name of our school system had gone before us.

Women's Ministry

In addition to education within the orbit of our school system, all corps were encouraged to set up women's literacy classes for those who had missed out on formal education. Some of these were very successful, particularly those at Gardnerville (Captain John Bundu) and the Chapel corps (Lieutenant Momo Douwee).

At both these centres, classes developed so well that they could almost be classified as 'evening school' with mature women (plus an occasional elderly man) progressing through several elementary grades. Graduation ceremonies were held and the newly educated demonstrated their new skills by publicly reading from the Bible and other texts. Mostly, however, women were happy to reach the stage where they could write their own names when they visited the clinic and be sufficiently capable to do the simple calculations necessary for their petty trading. It is hard to describe the pride and dignity that was given to a woman once she could sign her name, rather than just make her mark!

All corps, without exception, also organized certain women's activities under the title of 'Home League'. During the week women would have their own meeting in which aspects of education, worship, service and fellowship would be incorporated. While our work was restricted to Monrovia, Dorothy held sewing courses for these groups with second-hand sewing machines donated from friends in the UK. They had to be manual machines, of course, because there was no electricity. Threading and oiling them kept Dorothy doubly busy because of their age and variety of manufacturers.

In time each corps was given one and later, officer wives also received a machine. Other activities also included instruction in soap making, tie dying and HIV and AIDS prevention etc. The highlight of the home league's year was always their special Sunday, when a highly respected woman was crowned as 'Mother of the Year'. After the crowning ceremony, the Mother would then oversee a fundraising effort that would be very productive and on most occasions extremely humorous. The event was, of course, rounded off with a communal meal. In the early days I became very adept at the task of making the crowns from card board and kitchen aluminium foil!

CHAPTER 6

Bullets Start to Fly – October 1992

We had been back from our first furlough in 1992 for just two months when we were shocked to hear shooting coming from outside our house.

As we peered out we saw one of the tall Senegalese soldiers looking down the sights of his rifle. He was standing on the upstairs balcony of the building opposite our house, shooting down the street. The rebels had begun their new advance to take over the capital, and had been infiltrating steadily for the past months. Soldiers were moving along the street, shooting as they went. Then there was a booming sound that shook the house.

What it was we only found out a few hours later. Ghanaian war ships off the Liberian coast were firing over our house into the swamps beyond, where the main army of rebel troops was seeking to penetrate into the city. We ducked down in case stray bullets came our way, praying that the Senegalese troops, who were based in the former Russian Embassy alongside our house, would be able to repel Charles Taylor's men. Later we learnt that Taylor had code named this attack on Monrovia 'Octopus' as it was an advance on Monrovia using many different entry points.

When we took over our new house we believed that the Senegalese troops outside our door would be a strong defence because they were well disciplined soldiers. However, there was a negative side to their presence too. It seems they became a target for rebels to shoot at. It was not long before rockets were passing over our roof. You could hear them as they passed overhead and recognise the hiss that followed when they landed in the sea just a hundred yards from us. We were never quite sure what the best thing to do was once we heard rockets coming. Should we stand still, lay on the ground, or run?

I suspect in reality it was probably too late to do anything. Fortunately those firing the rockets and mortars were not well trained and none landed on us or the soldiers next door.

On our return to Liberia after a month's furlough in the UK we were eager to move the work forward outside of Monrovia. However, one of the things we needed to do was to set up home again. Before we left for our furlough we knew our lease on the apartment would have run out by the time of our return. We had, therefore, leased an unfurnished house. Back in the UK we had bought the furnishings which we knew we could not buy in Liberia and had put them, along with as many accessories as we could, into a container. Crucially, it also contained a generator. This was supposed to arrive within two or three weeks of our return.

While waiting for it to come we slept on an air bed and used a couple of wooden chairs with a very basic wooden table, borrowed from Tony Hage. We still had the gas cooker we obtained while in the apartment and gas, for a few more months, was obtainable The container arrived just a few days before the outbreak of fighting and for the next few weeks we had to face the possibility that all of it could have been lost; either to looters, if we had to find a safer location, or by fire, if a rocket had landed on us. It may sound strange but I think at the time we were more concerned at losing the Salvation Army's property than we were of injury to ourselves.

Soon after our return to Monrovia, just prior to Octopus, I managed to take a trip to Buchanan, the second city and port of Liberia. It was the first time I had ventured outside of the city. I didn't take Dorothy; instead I took a new convert, Jackson Towah, with me. In future days he was to play a vital role in the spread of the church outside of Monrovia, as well as being valuable to us in innumerable ways.

When we reached Buchanan we went to look at our church and to see if we could make contact with any Salvationists. The church building was a properly constructed, purpose-built structure that had almost been completed when the rebels took over the city in 1990. All that had been left to complete the building was its roof and I had paid the builder to do that as soon as we arrived in Liberia. We found the church intact with the roof properly completed, but to our surprise we didn't find a single Salvationist. We returned back, the same day.

Once back in Monrovia I began to make plans to send an officer out to Buchanan. Lieutenant Ben Gaymo and his wife, Etta, were both from the Bassa tribe, the same as most of the people in Buchanan, so they seemed the right people to send.

I did this believing that peace was on its way; I should have known better! The calm I had felt on returning from the UK was simply that which comes before a storm. Little did we realize that we would not see the lieutenants for another eighteen months. The attack, code named 'Octopus', on Monrovia took place less than six weeks after they moved to Buchanan. It took just a few days of fighting for the rebels to again take control of Buchanan.

People fled from that city, including our two Lieutenants. We learned later that they had been separated but that eventually each had reached their home villages where they waited and, when it was safe to do so, held services with the local people. Salvationists all over the world were praying for them and their prayers were heard.

After a few months ECOMOG troops recaptured Buchanan and I heard there were regular checkpoints on the road, so we decided to go and see if we could get any news of the Gaymos and other Salvationists. This time Dorothy went with us. It was rather a tense drive because we knew there were still pockets of rebel soldiers hiding in the dense undergrowth; we almost anticipated being ambushed round every bend in the road. Jackson had put a small Salvation Army flag on the front of the vehicle to make us look more official but we had not expected the reaction that it provoked.

As we approached an ECOMOG base and checkpoint soldiers came rushing out of their tents and resting places. They were hurrying to get dressed properly, including trying to find their helmets. It had been announced earlier in the week that a senior United Nations official was to pass that way sometime during the week and we had been mistaken for him. I don't know who was the most embarrassed, the soldiers or us. Fortunately it was a Ghanaian contingent of soldiers and the senior man knew the Salvation Army from his own country, so we were not given a hard time before being allowed to carry on with our journey.

In Buchanan we found a few Salvationist, as people were just beginning to return back to their homes from their hiding places in the bush. Most needed food, medicines and clothing because they had lost everything when they had fled from the rebels. A promise was given that we would return as soon as we could gather some relief supplies to bring to them. I did, however, explain to them that our resources were small. Returning several times, we brought them basic medicines, used clothing and a small amount of rice and milk powder.

It was a great relief to find that the church building was still intact and even its roof had not been damaged. There was, however, no news about the whereabouts of the Gaymos. However, a year and a half later, as tensions lessened, Ben found his way back to Monrovia and with the help of a little cash, it was not long before Etta was reunited with her husband and colleagues in Monrovia. They were both weak but were back to full health and strength within a short while. When eventually it was believed to be safe again in Buchanan, the Gaymos returned there, as divisional officers, both being promoted to the rank of captain. By this time other corps in Bassa villages, such as Trodain (Ben's home village), Kporyor (Etta's Home) and Dorsohn had been holding regular services again as well as in Buchanan.

On the way back from Buchanan we passed the Robertsfield International Airport which is almost 40 miles from Monrovia. The long runway, built by the Americans, still looked in good condition but the terminal buildings were all in ruins. We wondered if we would one day be privileged to see it brought back to life again; possibly have the pleasure of taking off from that long runway.

The first half of the road back to the capital passes through semi wooded areas with several villages close to the road but after passing through Cotton Tree, and Harbel (the hub of the Firestone Rubber Company) there is very little sign of habitation close to the road. Clearly, when the road from the airport was built the road route chosen was the most convenient for the international travellers, not the local inhabitants. There are some palm trees and a few other types of tree but these were at least a hundred yards from the road. Mostly the land was uncultivated with short grass.

Just outside of the airport we had to pass through a small town known as 'Smell No Taste'. I think it was given this name when people were constructing the airport. Either the workers could smell but not eat the villager's food or it was the other way round. The road from the airport to within a few miles of Monrovia was good, and much better than from Buchanan to the airport. Every hundred yards or so there was a burnt out car or an abandoned military vehicle,reminders to us that we were still in a war zone. As we approached Monrovia the road increasingly became pitted with potholes; a consequence of the war and lack of maintenance on a road taking a heavy load of traffic, made up mostly of military vehicles.

It seems that the attack on Monrovia in October, 1992, was not totally unexpected by the ECOMOG forces but for us and most of the aid agencies it was an unpleasant surprise.

Many expatriates working in the country started to evacuate and even chartered planes for their personnel to depart on. Some Americans offered us a place on one of these planes, but we decided we would stay, even though the British Foreign Office was advising all British personnel to leave as soon as possible. This was no great surprise to us; before we had left England, even then they were telling everyone that they should not go to Liberia.

In some parts of the city the rebels had gained ground and there were pockets of them in buildings from which they fired on soldiers and civilians. These were mostly people who had infiltrated in previous months and didn't show themselves until Taylor's forces began their advance on the city.

ECOMOG soldiers told us that there had been hundreds, possibly thousands, of child soldiers placed in the front line of the attacking forces. Taylor's generals knew that mature soldiers would often pause before shooting at children. That moment of hesitation could prove fatal for them. Child soldiers simply attacked ECOMOG and government forces head-on and without fear, blazing away with their automatic guns (mostly AK 47's). It was commonly believed they were given drugs to aid their courage, and sometimes they carried charms and talismans with an incantation that was supposed to make them immune to bullets.

Many child soldiers were killed in this assault on the city and hundreds more were captured. Some became detached from their comrades and simply fled into the city where they mingled with the crowds who had flooded into the city for protection. This led to many dreadful scenes where city youths, acting as vigilante soldiers, killed youths in the street who they suspected were rebels. Mostly this was done simply on the basis that they had certain ceremonial cut marks on their face or bodies which linked them to the tribes fighting or aligned to Taylor's army.

Three of our young lads in their middle teens, Eric Jackson, Eric Walker and Samuel Jubor, from our Bushrod Island corps, decided to travel to our house for safety. This was because most of the real fighting was taking place on their side of the town. As they approached the bridge to cross over to down town Monrovia, they were stopped by a group of these vigilantes. Eric Jackson was targeted by them because he had some of those tell-tale tribal scars. He was made to open his mouth and a rifle was placed in it. There was little doubt that they were about to execute him on the spot.

Jubor and Walker began to cry, fearing this would be the end of their friend but just then an ECOMOG soldier grabbed the gun and admonished the self-appointed judge, jury and executioner. Our boys hurried on, leaving the soldier to lecture the vigilante. When they arrived at our house, all three were suffering shock and trauma. The first thing we did was to give them a hot and very sweet cup of tea before they almost hysterically, and with a flood of tears, narrated what had happened to them on the way.

With soldiers, vigilantes and an occasional band of rebels out on the streets it wasn't safe for them to return for almost three weeks, during which time they camped in our large laundry room and we kept them supplied with food.

We did have a security guard, called Lawson Warbey, at the onset of this insurgency and he too became trapped in our compound. As there was very little for him to do Dorothy decided to teach him how to type. This was when we discovered that he was a clever young man, for he learned very quickly. Once things died down in the city we invited him to our City Church, which he responded to and started to attend there regularly.

Eventually he committed himself to the Lord, which meant a considerable change in his life-style. Within a short time he was made the registrar of the Len Millar High School and The Salvation Army helped him to attend the Liberia University to obtain an Associate Degree in Accounting and Business Management.

When the 'Liberia Region' became a 'Command' in January, 1997, I became responsible for all records and accounts. Previously, our records and receipts were passed on to Ghana Territory. Up to that time it was Ghana's responsibility to sort out the details from my cash sheets and put them into ledger format. Now we were a Command, all accounts had to be held by us and recorded as double entry accounts.

I had guessed when I was sent to Liberia that this was likely to happen but when I asked for a few lessons in standard bookkeeping I had simply been given a book of instructions. Needless to say, I had not mastered any of it. So I called in Lawson and made him the Command accountant. He had just completed his Associate Degree in Accounting and together we worked hard at making sense of the mysteries of double entry bookkeeping. We were enormously relieved when, after about a year, our International Headquarters in London sent Major Margaret Castely out for two weeks to train us. She was a good teacher and we learned a lot from her.

When we finally left Liberia, Lawson was still faithfully fulfilling that role. He has proved himself loyal and reliable, as well as a quiet but sincere Christian. I could not have done without him and it all begun when he was trapped in our compound at the time of Taylor's 1992 assault on Monrovia. I never cease to wonder at the way God does provide for our needs and the requirements of his work in personnel, as well as material matters.

Within a few weeks of the NPFL rebel forces being repulsed and turned back from the streets of Monrovia another military faction appeared which was opposed to Charles Taylor's men. This militia was called ULIMO and it soon split into a 'J' and a 'K' faction.

Initially, many hoped they would support the government forces and overwhelm Taylor's men, bringing the war to a swift conclusion. It was soon discovered, however, that ULIMO had their own agenda. For a time there were some very strange sights on the streets because soldiers started appearing wearing ladies' wigs and at times even ladies' dresses. We were also saddened to see some really young child soldiers with them, sometimes carrying guns as tall as themselves. Eventually ECOMOG had them cleared off the streets, but it left us with the realization that we were indeed now living in both a dangerous and unique situation.

Once it was safe for us to go back onto the streets to do some shopping, we were surprised to see tanks at various places along the road and numerous road blocks. The tanks were mostly pointing with their backs to the sea and their guns toward the swampland. Things did not die down all of a sudden, and you could never be sure that the firing of rockets and mortars would not begin again. On our first Sunday out we went over to Bushrod Island for the service, and while we were holding it a rocket landed in the field of the school in which we were worshipping. The congregation seemed to take it as normal, so we simply continued. As we left the area, we discovered a mortar had also landed in the garden of a house just fifty yards from the school and by the side of the road on which we had passed to come and go to the service.

We could see that the damage and danger had been much greater on the Bushrod Island side of town than where we were living. Many homes had been destroyed and large numbers of people had been displaced. They were now living in school buildings closer to the centre of town.

We heard that one of the boys who had attended our first meeting at the school, Ernest Ross, was sick and living with his step mother in one of these centres. When we found him he had sores round his mouth and over a lot of his body. It was also obvious that he had been living in the same clothes for a long time. We returned later with some ointment, clothes and a few bars of soap, plus sweets. The following Sunday we were surprised to see him making his way to church; a walk of about mile and a half. For a sick 12 year old boy, in tropical heat, this was an encouraging sign of real commitment. As with Jackson, this lad was, in future years, to play a significant role in the development and expansion of The Salvation Army's work in Liberia.

Following this outbreak in fighting, we made our first attempt to provide some relief assistance in Monrovia to those displaced by the rebel attacks. We only had US$2,000, which was a trivial amount in comparison to the need. But we felt we had to show our compassion for the suffering people so we bought boxes of soap (toilet and washing), tooth paste and slippers (flip flops worn by most Liberians instead of shoes). Using our most recent converts, we sent them into two of the schools that were housing displaced people. They really enjoyed distributing the supplies but didn't find it too easy to accept that they could have no more for themselves than they had been giving to others. It was a lesson they had to learn, for it was clear that most of the people giving out relief supplies in Liberia always made sure they had put aside a generous amount for themselves.

In the years that followed we did receive large amounts of clothes, shoes, blankets and soft toys which we tried to pass on to the corps for distribution where there was most need. But I used to tell the corps leaders that the 'devil' was in those bags, as they always brought out the worst in people. Even when the crowds who came to receive free handouts were managed in relatively good order, it was found that some people were taking more than the specified amount; some were passing items out through the windows to waiting relatives and others simply dressed quickly in items that could be easily worn.

Often there were arguments about who should receive what and it really surprised us when adult men demanded soft toys while they were being given out to the children. Worse still was the attitude of the village teachers who were aggrieved when it was explained to them that the allocation of milk powder being supplied was only to be given to youngsters on our malnourished children's feeding programme and not for adults.

It was not easy to find secure places to store goods that were for free distribution. In the early days we were limited to just one double garage, which was gradually increased by a container in the compound and then a second container. However, in spite of having at least one security guard on duty round the clock, things still disappeared. On one occasion we found that Patrick, the day security guard was going home looking rather fatter than he had arrived. On investigation it was discovered that he was wearing two pair of trousers (both different to the pair he had arrived in), three shirts, two jackets (pockets filled with socks and pants) and a new pair of shoes. There were other items stuffed up his shirt and in his pants. He must have been suffering because the temperature was about 33°C.

On another occasion we had noticed that the boxes of milk powder we had received from Switzerland seemed to be going down faster than they should. We didn't know how, until a friend of Ernest who lived up the road from HQ, told him that someone was driving the jeep out of the compound filled with boxes whenever we both went out at weekends. It could only have been the security guard but we didn't even know he could drive. So I decided to set a trap for him, knowing he would only deny it if he wasn't faced with cast-iron evidence.

We let it be known that we were going to a corps out of town and would probably not be back until the middle of the afternoon. Before leaving I recorded the reading of the mileage counter of the jeep. When we returned I checked the counter and felt the bonnet of jeep – it was warm and the reading had gone up by a distance of six miles.

We had the evidence. When faced with the warm engine, he said he had just sat in the cab and turned the engine over. He had no explanation for the additional mileage. Sadly he had to be sacked, as were all employees caught stealing. We lost some good men because they could not resist the temptation to steal. The milk powder was a huge temptation because it brought a high price when sold in the market. It seemed strange to us that those who had been dismissed for stealing could not understand that being forgiven did not mean that they could have their jobs back.

In the political history of Liberia it was not at all uncommon for disgraced politicians to be reinstated after just a brief time in prison; so why should common people expect to be treated any differently?

There were numerous aid agencies working in Liberia, many of them dealing with the distribution of food from the World Food Programme, the European Common Market and the United Nations. Various Roman Catholics overseas groups were also prominent in feeding programmes, particularly for those who gathered around their hospitals and clinics. We did not get deeply involved with the distribution of food. On a few occasions we did buy rice to distribute at displaced camps when we heard of real hardship. This was at times when other agencies for one reason or another were lacking supplies. On other occasions, the food we delivered was given mainly for family groups who were in towns suffering from an influx of displaced people from the interior.

All our city and town corps were asked to set up a team of people, called a League of Mercy. They used to circulate in the district around the church to discover the households that were suffering the most. Then the head of these homes would be given a ticket and a time to collect rice and cooking oil. This seemed the best way to use our meagre resources of money and of manpower. The procedure was always carried out by volunteers.

One exception to this was when we received a consignment of tinned food in a container from the UK. It included a ton of tinned vegetable soup, one of beans and another of carrots. Added to this were hundreds of packets of macaroni. At this time there was a displaced camp full of elderly people near to our corps at Salala. A message was sent out to the camp for them to come and collect the food. The beans and the soup didn't present any problem and even macaroni was known to most of them, but strange to say, most didn't know what carrots were. But one of the helpers quickly informed them that it was like pumpkin and they all went away happy with their arms full, with the additional gift of a small amount of milk powder.

Some of these tins and packets were stored at our head quarters along with some small bags of rice and boxes of milk powder gratefully received from the Swiss Government and passed on to us by the Swiss Salvation Army. These were very useful for the many occasions when people came begging. We had to be careful with callers saying that they were desperate, as Liberians, we soon discovered, were very good storytellers. On one occasion a man came to the HQ saying he, along with his wife and child, had been running from trouble in the interior. With tears in his eyes he went on to explain that a vehicle had brought him into town, a mile away, but the driver would not let him have any of his goods until he had paid the full fare for such a trip. He needed another L$500 (about US$15 at that time) before his belongings would be released. In a pitiful way he went on to say his wife was sick. He sounded very credible and certainly appeared to be in great distress.

However, I gave the cash to Jackson and told him to go with him to sort things out. A hundred yards up the road the man turned round to Jackson, admitted that there was no family and goods waiting to be released and offered to share the cash fifty-fifty with him. Much to his surprise, Jackson turned round immediately and brought the cash back to me.

Not long after the 'Octopus' attack had died down we were able to purchase a large house for our Headquarters just 25 yards from the beach. After several adaptations we occupied part of the upstairs space and left all the ground floor for headquarters business, which by then was increasingly employing more people. In many ways the building suited our needs very well, but it didn't take us long to discover that the contractors employed to repair the roof before we occupied it had not done a good job.

The move was just one hundred yards down the road and fortunately it was down hill slightly. With great difficult we managed the job of transferring all our furniture and other items into the new building. It had not been easy because we had no truck to carry things in, so our workers and friends had to carry everything on their heads, which included armchairs and settees.

The major task, however, was the moving of the generator. With extreme care, four of our workers managed it by rolling it down the street on tubular metal poles. Getting it into the compound was especially difficult, but by rolling and levering the generator eventually reached its appointed place without being damaged. That night we went to bed tired but relieved and pleased at what had been achieved. Our joy didn't last for long, however. That night we had one of the terrible October storms; the winds coming off the Atlantic Ocean with tremendous force and thunder and lightning the like of which can only be seen and heard in the tropics. Next morning we discovered that some of the roof had not received the new asbestos sheets that had been paid for.

The house was now an island, completely surrounded by water and floating on it were lots of pieces of old asbestos sheeting from the roof. When we later went onto the beach and looked back at our roof, it was easy to see where the old sheets had not been exchanged for new ones as they were a different colour. In the end we got used to such storms in October with the need to have a few asbestos sheets ready to replace those blown away.

CHAPTER 7

Let's Get Planting (Churches)

We have already explained how we found just one Salvation Army corps, Sinkor, holding services when we first arrived in Monrovia, with Lieutenants Ben and Etta Gaymo as its officers. Then we revived Bushrod Island Corps and brought in Lieutenant Matthew Dogbah as its officer. Once these corps seemed to be moving along quite well we started to look around for other districts within Greater Monrovia for us to establish more.

It was still too dangerous to venture far outside of the city. The obvious first place to look was Paynesville. Technically it was Paynesville City but to people who didn't live there it was a large bustling suburb to the north-east of Monrovia which appeared like one huge market. For much of our first five years in Liberia it was also the outer limit of the jurisdiction and authority of the various interim governments who administered Greater Monrovia; the only land not occupied by rebel factions.

Finding a suitable centre to start a church was not easy. We could find nothing in the heart of Paynesville so had to settle for the Community School, in the Joe Bar district. This was about a mile from the main market and shopping district of Paynesville, usually called the red light district, not because of the abundance of street women but because there had once been traffic lights at the road junction.

For a few weeks Lieutenant Gaymo tried to open a corps in the afternoon, following his morning service at Sinkor. The response was minimal. However, with Lieutenants Dogbah installed at Bushrod Island, my wife and I were free on Sunday mornings to go out to Paynesville to try opening a corps at a time of day more closely associated with worship services. It was here that my cornet became very helpful. I used to stand in front of the school and play some hymns which I hoped might be recognized as such. To start with there were just three of us standing there: my wife and me, plus one teenaged boy. He was the only firm contact Lieutenant Gaymo had made. We would then cross the street to speak with the people who had been looking at us – I hesitate to say 'listening to us'.

Each week the numbers gathering for worship slowly grew until we were averaging around forty adults and twenty or so children, so we sent for the last couple of Liberians who had been trained in Ghana. Sadly, shortly after handing the corps over to them there was a problem between the members and the officers. It seems people felt he was being too authoritarian. Unfortunately the wife, though a kind person, had been allowed to train without the ability to read properly. There were several other complications with this couple and after a while, following a transfer to Sinkor Corps, their officership was terminated.

Several different venues were used for Paynesville Corps including the home of one of its members, Mr. John Kokulu, who later became the first Principal of the William Booth High School. By the end of 1997 the school auditorium had been built and Paynesville Corps took up residence in its present building. For a while, prior to its move to the school campus, the young man, Jackson Towah, was made an envoy in charge of the corps. Amongst other things, he actively evangelised among the workers on the building site. This proved productive even before the final move, so when services began on the William Booth campus there was already a congregation of about fifty adults and thirty children. This grew rapidly once the school was opened as many teachers and students made it their spiritual home.

Captain Barromi Davis had an interesting and testing experience soon after he was appointed to Paynesville. He was a kind and compassionate officer but his dog bit his neighbour and in spite of offering to take his neighbour to the clinic and pay any and all medical expenses he was arrested and imprisoned in Monrovia Central police station. It was a spiteful and vindictive act by someone who bore a grudge against The Salvation Army. The prison was a dreadful place where cells could contain more than a dozen inmates, several of whom were likely to be murderers. By the time I heard about it and sent someone to bail the captain out, he had been incarcerated for two days; not long but long enough to have possibly been severely harmed both physically and mentally. But it didn't happen that way at all; as the person sent to pay the bail money soon discovered.

Down the corridor of the jail there resonated strange sounds which were gradually distinguished as the raucous singing of '*He's got the whole world in His hands*'. The captain had them all singing religious songs and choruses, and the previous evening he had read his Bible and prayed with them. I couldn't help but smile, as it reminded me of the jail at Philippi with the singing of Paul and Silas.

Mention has already been made of Bushrod Island Corps which grew out of those initial open-air services. Several of the first members from there went on to be pioneers at the next Corps,

Monrovia City. Others had got saved at our Mamba Point quarters, and to start with they preferred to travel over to the Bushrod Island Corps where we worshipped in English, rather than to attend Sinkor Corps which was orientated toward Bassa in language and style of worship. When in January 1993 the Barnes building (formerly occupied by the Youth and Sport ministry) was refurbished, Monrovia City Corps was opened on the ground floor of the school building. Several Salvationists from Bushrod Island and from Sinkor joined us for the open-air service at the local market and then marched back with us to the school. Those from Bushrod Island who lived in the south-east of the city then transferred to the City Corps. This was just one of the factors which led to its rapid growth. The adaptation of the school had attracted a lot of attention from the general public, and this was another factor, which encouraged many people to attend as well as the desire of some to become teachers at the school.

In our first year in Liberia, while living in our Mamba Point apartment, the owner decided to add a second floor to the building. This gave us another opportunity to make contact with people and to share the Gospel. The masons, painters and plumbers, who had been working on the building, were mostly part of one extended family and they were very curious about us and our church. This friendship had led us to invite them to do most of the renovation work on the Barnes building. When they completed the work they also accepted our invitation to join us in worship, together with their families. It was a promise they had volunteered before they had started the work and we were happy when we saw them keep their promise. The school and the corps opened in January, 1993, and in 1995 a large, well constructed church was built, alongside the Municipal City Hall, with many of the same team of workers. It was constructed so quickly that several people said they thought it was prefabricated. These same workers later became founding members of the Corps at Gardnersville, a suburb of Monrovia and their home district.

Right from the start Salvation Army history and doctrine were taught alongside the normal Bible Knowledge classes in our schools. The result has always been to attract students as well as staff to The Salvation Army from our schools. My wife and I ran the City Corps until the August of that year, when Lieutenants Wheigar returned from training in Ghana and took charge of it. After a year or so the Wheigars were transferred to Paynesville Corps and for the following six years my wife and I again took charge of the City Corps in addition to all our other duties!

Gardnersville Corps was opened in April 2003 after we had held just a few open-airs services and was then led by Brother William Sackie, one of the three attendees at that first meeting we had ever held at Bushrod Island in November 1991. The work here took off quickly because, as I have mentioned, those workers who joined us at worship in the early days at the City Corps transferred to Gardnersville Corps as it was close to where they lived. In October 1993, William, with Doris his wife, went to train as officers in Ghana. At that time we still had no training facilities in Liberia; we were just a 'Region' under the jurisdiction of the Ghana Territory.

In our first two years we had managed to establish five new churches, making a total of six in Monrovia. The sixth was at St. Paul Bridge. This was one of the poorer and needier areas on the north-western edge of Monrovia. Two members of the Sinkor Corps lived there, travelling across the city every Sunday for worship.

My wife and I, helped by a converted former child soldier, Benedict Miapeh, started to hold open-air gatherings for the children and followed this up by visiting their parents. We also distributed some milk powder from Canada to that community for we saw that many of the children were malnourished. Benedict lived in that district and I had made contact with him on our first visit. He started to attend our Bushrod Island church and got converted. With his help and that of the two Salvationists from Sinkor, a small corps was successfully started. It took a little while to make much progress, but it is now well established. Lieutenant and Mrs. Youngar were its first officer leaders.

It was a great joy on one of our later visits there to be able to enrol sixteen new soldiers, fourteen of whom had come up through its young people‘s department.

Mention has already been made of our Bassa Corps and the delay caused by the fighting to get them gathering for worship and giving them leaders. The same was true of the few small Gola/Kpelle speaking churches.

Early in 1993, when things became a little safer around Monrovia, we ventured out to Fendale University campus where several thousand displaced people were being housed. Word had reached us that it was where the family looking after Cadet Youngar's children were staying. Having heard they were desperately in need of the clothing, food and medicines we took what we could for them. Sadly, when we got there we found the baby that the cadets had left behind, before travelling to Ghana for training, had died.

About six months later we heard there were about thirty Salvationist families from corps in Grand Bassa County who had found their way to a displaced persons' camp in Buchanan. This was after ECOMOG had, recaptured the town. We were very surprised that the Gaymos were not included in this number.

Several trips were organised, taking food and used clothing to Buchanan but what were most appreciated were the anti-malarial drugs, worming tablets and a variety of other pain-relieving tablets such as paracetamol and aspirin. Using this quiet time we also sent word to Gowingbo Church that we would bring some supplies for them to the Buchanan side of the river that separates them from the port. When we arrived we were surprised to find that about twenty members had crossed the river and were waiting in a Baptist church for us. Getting the boxes back to Gowingbo meant transporting them over the swift flowing river on dug-out canoes; a very dangerous task, but all was successfully and safely accomplished. I was relieved to know that we did not have to take the canoe crossing as by the next time we visited Gowingbo we had found an alternative route by dirt road.

Shortly after 'Octopus' another advance was made on Monrovia with rebel forces attacking from the Paynesville district. This happened in the early hours of Sunday morning. I hadn't heard about this, so Dorothy and I set off for our corps at Paynesville where we were due to conduct the morning service. Once we reached the Boulevard it quickly became obvious that we were heading in the wrong direction. Hundreds of people were traipsing toward the centre of town with their foam mattresses on their heads, some carrying large bundles and others with wheelbarrows. Clearly there was trouble ahead but we continued going forward, but at a slower pace as we thought our officers might need a lift into town. When we reached our church leaders we found they were content to stay where they were, for it seemed that the attack had been more a looting party than a real invasion. No one turned up for the service so we turned round and returned home, content to know that our leaders had not been harmed.

Apart from the five new churches we had opened in Monrovia during the first two or three years of our activities in Liberia, our main efforts were to revive those churches that had existed before the civil war. As well as the Bassa churches this included the Gola and Kpelle-speaking congregations at Menigay, Mount Coffee, Clean Town and Gull Nee. We travelled to them whenever ECOMOG would give us a pass, which was not often. Seldom was it deemed safe enough for civilians to move out of Monrovia until late 1996. Even after that time there were long periods when we became pinned down in Monrovia or could only go to 'safe' areas. Usually we took some relief supplies which included clothing, food and medicines but most of all we went with the 'Word' and with prayer. It was clear that this did bring encouragement to our people and we were sad that we could not reach them more often.

These early days were not without problems. Even when we were trying to bring help to distressed people we could sometimes encounter barriers and at times there was strong opposition. One example of this was when we had been helping at a camp for displaced people, giving them top quality powdered milk from Switzerland. Some of the seriously malnourished people had been a little sick but that was because they took too much too quickly. We had warned them about such a reaction and explained how they should use the milk. To our surprise, however, an article appeared in one of the newspapers saying that we had been distributing out-of-date milk that was making people ill. It was of course a lie, but the editor of the paper wanted us to pay for him to print a rebuttal.

On another occasion, not long after 'Octopus' and while tension was still high, two phone calls were received by us on the same day. The caller said he had overheard soldiers at the barracks planning to commit armed robbery on our compound in the very near future. As you can guess, this did cause us some concern. However, while I was working at about midnight that same day, Dorothy came to me excitedly from the bedroom where she had been following her daily reading from 'Words of Life'. '*Look.*' she said, pointing at a page in the Bible she was holding. "*I think this must be God's reply to those phone calls.*" She began to read from Acts 18: 9-12 "*Keep it up, and don't let anyone intimidate or silence you. No matter what happens, I'm with you and no one is going to be able to hurt you.You have no idea how many people I have on my side in this city. That was all that was needed for him to stick it out in that city.*"(The Message)

And that's how it was also for us, though we did take reasonable precautions.

Initially, the most serious opposition, strangely enough, was actually from within the Army membership. I suspect the cause of this really relates back to the very beginning ofThe Salvation Army's activities in Liberia. Whenever members were invited to speak they invariably reeled off a long lists of 'wants'. It gave us the impression that the majority of people who had wanted The Salvation Army to incorporate them into the international movement had done so, to some degree, for materialistic reasons. I also feel that there was not a complete understanding as to how The Salvation Army organisation operates.

Added to which, some people had become soldiers without fully understanding our doctrine and how it differed from that to which they had known. Even some of the officers who had trained in Ghana expected The Salvation Army to be the provider of much more than was possible. This attitude took quite some time to moderate and for a while it was a hindrance to the progress of the work.

Probably the saddest illustration of this was when we opened the boys' hostel and gave former child soldiers a roof over their heads, food for their bellies and education for their minds. Some officers thought we were robbing them. They felt that these youths who had been fighting, and possibly killing, should not be helped. Even the fact that these youths had all responded positively to the Gospel message did not produce any charitable reaction from some of them. I just had to pray that the light would dawn on them one day.

It is a young church in Liberia; I had to believe that as spiritual maturity grew in our people greater understanding would also come. Sadly, while that understanding was growing we did lose a few officers and some soldiers.

This was not an easy time for us as some of the antagonism became very personal. It was then that we appreciated still being part of a larger territory for our Territorial Commanders, Colonels William and Eleanor Norris, were great encouragers. They also supported us when we had to make some key changes in officers and employees. This was important because we had no one to turn to in Liberia. All our officers were Liberians with only a very few years experience.

When the Command celebrated its tenth anniversary, in 1998, it was a joy for us to welcome the colonels back and to enjoy their fellowship and powerful ministry.

CHAPTER 8

Medical Work Calls

It was several years before we felt competent to start any official medical work on behalf of The Salvation Army. Schools had been something of which I had some knowledge, having had fourteen years experience as a teacher prior to my officership and four years in-charge of Bradley Mission School in Zimbabwe. Medicine, however, was something for which I felt I had no qualifications. The limit of my experience and knowledge in medicine had been gained at Bradley, where Dorothy and I conducted sick parade every morning with the help of "*Where There is No Doctor*", a book that many people on missionary service have found invaluable.

By the beginning of 1995, however, we sent Martha, who we first got to know when she was working as one of our cooks at the Len Millar School, to train as a nurse. By that time she had become a soldier at the City Corps.

A year later two young men, Cyrus and Mike, graduates of the Len Millar School, were also sponsored by the Army to train as Physician's Assistants (country doctors). By the time Martha had completed her training we were able to open our two clinics: one on the William Booth campus and the other as an extension to the church at St. Paul's Bridge. Mrs. Sarah Anokwuru, a soldier at Bushrod Island and an experienced BSc. nurse, became the first head of the St. Paul Clinic, while Mr. Nah, an experienced physician's assistant, and a Methodist, was made the Officer-in-Charge at the

William Booth Clinic. Naturally, once Martha and the two young men qualified they worked for the Army's medical services in Liberia.

One other smart young graduate from the Len Millar School, John Dogba, was trained as a laboratory technician. He was a highly valued asset to the William Booth Clinic until 2003 when the Army decided to sponsor him to become a doctor. He has now obtained a BSc in Biology and Chemistry, has been accepted for entry into the Medical School for 2010 and while he waits, is doing a Master's Degree in Public Health.

Emmanuel Urey left his father's rural home in his early teens because he wanted to get a secondary education. His father was a farmer, blacksmith and an active member of a traditional secret society. He wanted his son to follow in his footsteps. So Emmanuel took himself to the town of Gbarnga where he met the leader of The Salvation Army church in that town. Seeing that Emmanuel had great potential, he sent him to our boys' hostel in Monrovia. His father did not object. At first the hostel boys tended to joke with him and call him 'country boy' because he was very dark skinned. I was told that this is caused through having worked for a long time in his father's fields.

He had the last laugh, however, as he soon headed them all in academic achievement, going on to be the head boy at the Len Millar High School. He has since been sponsored to obtain a BSc in Chemistry and Biology and at the time of writing has almost completed his Master's in Public Health.

A third student receiving medical sponsorship is Jonathan Hart. His father, a medical doctor, was beheaded by the rebels at the start of the war. This was because he was a Nigerian and had worked closely with people in the government; including a former president of Liberia. (Jonathan's story is told in appendix 4).

Fortunately for Jonathan, he eventually found his way to the Salvation Army at Gardnersville where Lieutenant William Sackie, seeing he was severely traumatised, brought him to Headquarters with the request that he be admitted to the boys' hostel. At first he was very morose and extremely quick-tempered. He was a brilliant student but on several occasions he got near to being expelled because of his rages. I am happy to say that gradually he became socially adjusted and managed to complete his first degree whilst acting as secretary for the William Booth High School. He has already completed his first three years at Medical School and is now gaining clinical experience on the road to becoming a successful Doctor of Medicine. Jonathan also assists HQ a little with the distribution of medicines for our clinics.

Though these three sponsorships are long-term steps of faith, we believe that the future of The Salvation Army's medical work in Liberia will be assured and that it will become accepted as being of an excellent standard. Hearty thanks are owed to the generous sponsors of our three prospective doctors, all of whom come from the Salvation Army's scholarship and sponsorship programmes in Norway.

The clinics were set up with two physician assistants, a nurse, a midwife, a nurse-aide and a laboratory technician; along with a registrar, cashier, day and night security and a janitor. The buildings contained four recovery beds, two inspection rooms, a treatment room, registrar and cashier's offices, plus a pharmacy.

The first baby to be delivered at a Salvation Army clinic in Liberia was a boy at Catherine Booth Clinic (St. Paul Bridge) and they called him William Booth. As with the school system, we have tried, with only limited success, to get the clinics to cover their own running costs. This has not been easy, for the people living around our clinics are genuinely poor and we have to charge a small fee because medicines have had to be bought retail.

When the LURD forces entered Monrovia in 2003 they did so over the St. Paul River Bridge and as a consequence our officers had to be rescued and the clinic closed down for more than six months. The William Booth Clinic, however, was kept busy because for a time the school campus became a camp for Internally Displaced People, with nearly 5,000 people living there. This meant the clinic staff, augmented by those from St. Paul Bridge, were able to fulfil a great humanitarian role; where as other camps expected a proportion of I.D.P.'s to die, not one person, adult or child, died of disease on the W.B. campus during this period.

When we met with the camp officials they were full of praise for the clinic staff, and for the way Lieutenant Barromi Davis had organised everything so that sickness did not spread through the campus. Because some people arrived with wounds caused by the fighting P.A.'s and nurses had to carry out tasks for which they had not been fully trained, including successfully removing a bullet from the skull of a patient. At the end of the day there was nothing but praise and gratitude for the dedication of the clinic staff. During this time some financial support was obtained for the nurses and some free medicines given by an NGO. This ended as soon as the camp was closed.

Following this episode, aid-agencies who were operating their own clinics or pharmacies continued to give out medicines free of charge and it therefore became increasingly difficult to be completely self-sufficient because we had to lower our charges for medicines, laboratory testing and registration.

After the dramatic events of April 1996 we began gradually to move out into the interior and saw a great need for medical help and education. Dorothy began by taking Nurse Martha with her to give instruction in nutrition and baby care, as well as information about HIV and AIDS. They always took items like paracetamol, chloroquine and vermox tablets but quickly realised that more than this was required in the villages. They needed to be properly diagnosed and advised on the correct medicines and how to take them. It was clear too that they needed to be taught how to feed their babies properly, and what foods they themselves should be eating. It was then that we decided to set up a mobile clinic that would go into villages such as Menigay once a week, if possible, and other places on an irregular basis.

Martha was the first to oversight this work and over the years since 1997 the mobile clinic has gone out and performed a truly holistic function, starting with a time of prayer, the reading of the Word and some cheerful chorus singing. This would be followed with teaching on anything from hygiene to HIV and AIDS. Then clinics would be held. Usually they went out with a team of four or five: one P.A. to do diagnosing, a nurse to operate the makeshift pharmacy with the nurse-aid helping her with treatment. The driver acted as the registrar. Sometimes they could have as many as 120 patients to deal with in a day, and there were times when we got worried as the jeep had not arrived back before it got dark, around 7 pm. There was one spot on the mud road that often turned into a dangerously slippery slope, with a series of ruts deeper than the height of the jeep wheels.

On one occasion we had good cause to be concerned because the team had gone out to Todee District, which was known to be occupied by LURD forces, but the corps officer, who had returned there after having had all his belongings looted, had assured CHQ that they were friendly and were not interfering with vehicles passing through. The medical team reached their destination without incident and while they were holding clinic several militiamen came for treatment, politely waiting their turn. However, on the return trip a group of rebels on the road stopped them and forced the driver to take all of them to the rebel camp. They were fully aware that when they reached the camp it was quite possible that the man could be shot and the women raped. They also knew that even if they were spared, their vehicle was likely to be taken from them. To their great relief and surprise, once they reached the camp they were released without being harmed. Miraculously, their jeep was not taken from them either. They reached home badly shaken but otherwise unharmed.

Two things prevented a truly consistent work being carried out by the mobile clinic. One was the unreliability of the Land Rover jeep, and the other was those times when the districts surrounding Monrovia became infiltrated by various rebel factions. Nevertheless it was, and still is, extremely useful as the mobile clinic served various rural districts within a two-hour drive of the capital, plus several trips, on a one-off basis, even further, including Buchanan, Salala, Gbarnga and even Zwedru.

By the year 2000 a special feeding programme for malnourished babies and young children was commenced and conducted by the team out at Menigay, with the assistance of Captain Jesse Tar, the corps officer. This was done in a professional manner for a group of thirty children. It was begun with a survey to discover the true needs of the children in the area and involved the recording of height (length) and weight of those to be included in the project. These measurements were checked every two weeks after the children had received regular feeding by the officer of milk, cornmeal, sugar and oil. When one of the participants had reached an acceptable level of health and nutrition, they were replaced by another malnourished child. This work could have been multiplied many times but with our limited personnel, the problems with vehicles and costs, it was thought best to keep things within the resources of the Command.

In 2004 we changed from using a Land Rover jeep to a Toyota Land Cruiser jeep for our mobile clinic but within two months of it being on the road it was hit by a government lorry which was carrying crushed rock. No compensation was obtainable from the government even though it was assessed as a complete write-off and the lorry driver's fault. However, we did manage, at considerable expense, to have it repaired. When the accident happened, our vehicle was pushed into a house and landed up on its roof but miraculously the driver, Togbah Karpeh, climbed out of it shaken but without a scratch. It seems that, completely out of character, he had actually put on his seat belt (it is not compulsory in Liberia) and that saved him from going out through the windscreen to serious injury or even death.

This reminded us of another occasion when Oral Guanue, a former hostel boy, was driving some City Corps songsters to a mass songster practice. He took a bend too fast and rolled the jeep down an embankment. It rolled over twice and finished up on its wheels. People rushed to rescue what they assumed would be the seriously injured occupants, but the rear door opened and everyone stepped out with the worst casualty being a sprained ankle. Onlookers were heard to say "*God must really be in that church*". I say amen to that!

Of course, Dorothy and I were not immune to the diseases and infections that were rampant all over Liberia. Malaria was the most obvious danger because the land along the coast of Liberia is very swampy which, together with the tropical heat, made it an ideal breading ground for mosquitoes. Dorothy was meticulous with the necessary prophylactic drugs, so we probably were protected from the majority of mosquito assaults, but we still did suffer from Malaria several times. Often the Malaria did not respond to the normal treatment, so there were times when one or other of us was sat in bed attached to an I.V. drip which had to be hung from the overhead light fitting. Because of the pressure of work there were times when the employees had to be shown into my bedroom for them to receive instructions. This was particularly necessary for our building projects. On one occasion I also had Typhoid though it was not, thankfully, a very severe infection.

At least once when Dorothy was suffering from Malaria I was extremely worried as she did not respond to either the usual treatment or the alternative that was used. Fortunately there was a third choice of drug and to our immense relief Dorothy began to recover. It had been an anxious time for us as there had been little sign of recovery for more than a week. Infections don't always come at a convenient time either; like the time we were to host two auditors and Dorothy had only half recovered from a bout of Malaria.

I have suffered from Asthma since I was eleven years old so had come prepared with all my inhalers plus some steroids for emergencies. Although I did have a few minor attacks, I was seldom incapacitated. Thankfully, I think the steroids only had to come into play on a couple of occasions. This was quite remarkable in view of the many very stressful situations we had to pass through. Even when we were being attacked and having to flee from our quarters during the troubles of 1996 my asthma only troubled me slightly. That was when, on our way to the US Embassy, I tried to help load up the lorries with sacks of rice for the people sheltering in the camp on top of Mamba Point.

Before our own medical staff were trained it was much harder and more expensive to receive treatment, though quite early on we did find a very kind hospital doctor who was willing to call on us when we were sick. We were very grateful for the loving care we always received from our own medics: Martha, Cyrus, Mark and especially John (he was a real expert with the needle) who were always ready and willing to come to our assistance. It should be noted that we were always very careful to see that any needles used were taken from their original packaging as we didn't want to risk being infected with HIV/AIDS.

CHAPTER 9

Officer Training

Until 1998 there was no Officer Training College in Liberia; all Liberian cadets up to that time were therefore trained in Ghana. However, when Liberia was made a Command in 1997 serious attention was turned onto the possibility of training our own officers.

Once again we had to face the problem of suitable accommodation. It would have to include living quarters for cadets and an officer-couple as well as a classroom and a dining room with a kitchen. By the middle of 1998 a building in 18th Street was leased, not far from the headquarters in 17th Street. The building was not ideal in every respect but we could see, with some adaptations and refurbishment, it could be made to serve our purpose.

But we had no officer to run the college. We had already missed one year (1997) with no cadets in training so it was deemed important to get something started. Then news reached us that Majors Mavis and Raymond Mackereth had been appointed to the Command, with Ray to be the principal of the college as well as Command General Secretary. Mavis was appointed as house officer and teacher at the college. Shortly after the majors arrived, the 'Foward 2000' Session was started.

Unfortunately, after the college session had been running for just three months, rebels started to attack the city starting near St. Paul Bridge. Fearing that this time the rebels would get into the city, the majors returned to the UK to wait and see what was going to be the outcome. The rebels were repelled and the majors were able to return after six weeks enforced furlough. During this time Captain Sackie and his wife assisted me with the oversight of the college.

The session re-started with four couples and two single men. Sadly, it was discovered that one couple was not suitable because they had not been able to eradicate all former superstitious practices and beliefs from their lives. So, before the end of the first college year, they had to return to their home village. All the others went on to complete their training. One of them, Captain Okupuson Tawone, married Captain Mrs. Theresa Nimeley whose first husband had died when they were in training in Ghana. The wedding took place the day after he was commissioned. After the commissioning and ordination service, in July 2000, the Mackereths returned home where they were later made Regional Commanders in Rwanda.

One couple trained in this session was John and Rosalind Bundu. John had fled from the fighting in his own country, Sierra Leone, only to be arrested as a suspected spy when he entered Monrovia. However, after a few weeks of interrogation he was released. Knowing that John was a graduate teacher of English, the prison warder suggested he apply to become a teacher at the newly opened Salvation Army Len Millar High School. This he did, and we were happy to employ him as senior English instructor.

Within a year he had become a member of the Salvation Army and had applied to be considered for officership. But he had a wife, and she was still in Sierra Leone. In spite of many problems with communications, his wife Rosalind was contacted and she confessed that she had long felt that God was calling her to be a minister of the Gospel. This just left the difficulty of getting her to Monrovia, but with God's help, this was achieved.

One year later they entered the training college. Once commisioned and ordained, they not only served as corps officers, but played a big role in the next two training sessions. On 1 December 2009, Captains John and Rosalind were officially appointed to open the work ofThe Salvation Army back in their own country, Sierra Leone.

By the November we had started the next session of cadets without a principal so Captain Sackie, Captain B. Davis and Captain J. Bundu all assisted in the college programme. Help was on the way, however, as Major Pamela McKee from USA Eastern Territory, arrived just before the visit of General Gowans in January 2001. Shortly before her arrival we purchased a property in 18th Street, which we converted into our new training college. It did need to be adapted to meet the requirements of the college which included: six double rooms for the cadets, bathrooms and a large classroom. The first floor was able to be converted into a fine two-bedroom apartment for the Principal. A kitchen was then added outside in the yard with a large palaver hut for eating and, at times, for classes. Fortunately it had a generator house and a well, though this had to be refurbished and have the addition of a high level water tank added, together with a pump. The cadets moved into the new college after Easter 2001.

At the conclusion of the first college year the cadets all went off to Zwedru for their out-training. There they helped with the physical preparation of the land for a proposed new school, took part in person-to-person evangelism and led services and Bible studies. On their return, two couples were informed that they would not be staying another year to complete their studies. It had been decided that the husbands would be commissioned as lieutenants and given appointments; the reason for this was that the women did not come up to the required standard, both academically and in spiritual maturity.. It was pleasing to see that both couples accepted this, and the men went on to do good service with the support of their wives..

The Training Principal, Major Pamela McKee, did a valiant work with this second session of cadets for she had to do most of the work single-handed. Apart from the day-to-day teaching and training throughout the two years, she was daring enough to use her natural artistic talent to produce a musical drama. This was based on John Gowans' 'Glory' cleverly scripted to be likened to 'West Point', a rather rough fishing quarter of Monrovia. Church members from the City and Paynesville Corps joined with the cadets to give a uniquely special performance on the eve of the commissioning and ordination of the cadets.

Our third session of cadets started in February 2003 with three couples and four single men who, with the exception of one couple, all had previous experience of church leadership. The session had only been in progress for a couple of months when there was serious trouble. My wife and I were on furlough at the time.

The rebel militia, called LURD, entered Monrovia over the St Paul River Bridge. They moved forward onto Bushrod Island and began to bombard the centre of the city with rockets and mortars. The

Principal, Major Pamela McKee, was advised to evacuate and she flew out to Ghana where she was found some secretarial duties while awaiting calm to be restored to Monrovia. I was very happy when she was able to return to us in November.

Meanwhile the cadets stayed at the college and were well looked after by the efforts of Captains John Bundu and Solomon Jallayu as well as Mrs. Bainda (kitchen supervision/ dietician) and Lawson (Command accountant).

No harm came to any cadet but when I got back in August (as soon as a cease-fire was declared) I found them making demands to which the Command could not accede. The atmosphere at the college did not improve and in the end I decided that it would have to be closed temporarily while the source of the problem was found and remedied. The cadets had to leave the college and then apply to be reaccepted. The two couples who were thought to be at the root of the problems and one single man did not reapply. The rest did and were accepted.

The final outcome was that a new session was constituted with one of the cadets being allowed to marry and two new couples joining the group. This resulted in a session of four married couples and two single men. The college was opened as a new session and Major McKee began lectures at the beginning of February, 2004.

When, later in the year, the cadets went on out-training, all but one couple went in charge of a church or new opening and everyone of them performed exceedingly well, a sign to us that the right decisions had been made with respect to the re-accepted cadets.

CHAPTER 10

Child Soldiers Need a Home

Boys' Hostel

When in October, 1992, Charles Taylor's rebels attacked the city of Monrovia (Operation Octopus), the advance was actually led by child soldiers.

They did this because even a hardened soldier can hesitate before shooting a ten-year-old boy. But the boy does not wait; he fires indiscriminately without any conscience about who he is likely to harm. Of course many of these children (mostly boys in Liberia) were killed. Hundreds of others were captured and interned in the 'Beach Prison' where murderers were normally sent.

Jackson and I, plus one or two other Salvationists, went there and were permitted to evangelise and to distribute clothing. It is hard to describe the pitiful state of these boys, yet when we held a service they would all gather around and sit on the floor to listen to what we had to tell them. They also sang their hearts out for us, enjoying such choruses as "*When we all get to heaven what a day of rejoicing there will be*" and "*Soon and very soon, we are going to see the King*". Few of them would have seen the irony of singing such words in prison but some did get saved for we made altar calls just as we would have done in a church.

When, after almost a year of internment, these boys were finally released, some of them faced us with a big problem for, search as we might, we could seldom find any relative for them. This was because those attacking the capital had come from country districts often many miles away from Monrovia and at that time travel outside of the city was not possible. It was then that I decided to rent a couple of rooms for two or three of these boys. We called it a 'hostel' rather than a 'home' because they had to manage on their own with as little help from HQ as possible. We provided clothing, food and beds etc. but they had to do their own washing, cooking and buying of food.

These boys were not blood-thirsty sadistic killers. Some had joined Taylor's army believing they were fighting for a just cause. That was certainly true for Samuel Morgan, the captain of a small boys' unit. Given the nick-name 'Mosquito' he was, we found out later, very considerate toward civilians caught up in the fighting. The owner of our first Len Millar property told us that when Samuel's unit occupied her compound, as his unit advanced on Monrovia, he had actually shared his food with her.

Some of the older boy soldiers who were captured were taken to the athletes' accommodation by the stadium where they had to attend rehabilitation classes. I was invited to go there once a week to give them some counselling and Bible teaching. I used to take Jackson with me as he was the same age as them. Not all of them were Christians but none seemed to mind listening and discussing spiritual matters from a Christian point of view. After the class one or two of them would come to us for more personal spiritual guidance. It was from there that we met Oral and Guinness.

So our first three hostel boys were Samuel Morgan, Guinness Morris (who quickly changed his name to Abednego) and Oral Guanue. All of them were sent to the Len Millar School, where

Abednego and Oral graduated. Samuel dropped out because he was not academically minded so he was put onto building and carpentry courses. Oral also had some tailoring skills so for a long time he was the command tailor, sewing all our epaulettes and making school uniforms for both hostels. After graduating at the Len Millar High School he went on to the University of Liberia.

Emmanuel David joined the hostel when Samuel Morgan recognised him as one of his former boy soldiers. Emmanuel was washing up dishes at a cook-shop to earn a bowl of rice. He had been co-opted as a ten-year-old child soldier, assisting a rebel soldier guarding the port gates in Buchanan. As one of Samuel's 'boys' he had taken part in 'Octopus'. Somehow he had avoided being shot or captured and just merged into the city crowds. He not only went on to graduate from High School but became a good cornet player and a great athlete, running the 100 metres internationally. After showing great leadership skills during a team crisis in Benin he was made the captain of the national athletics team. Following his school graduation, the command sponsored him to go to Ghana. There he trained with Ralph Quiah, another hostel boy whose parents had been killed in the war, for ten months as computer hardware technicians. Both returned and continued to be active in the church.

Another orphan accepted into the boys' hostel was Sam Pewu. His mother had died soon after giving birth to his young sister and so he was being brought up by his father. Before the war his father had been one of only three policemen in Liberia to have been trained in finger-print analysis. He had been one of the first to be made a soldier at the City Corps and it wasn't long before he was made church secretary, as well as a teacher at the Len Millar School.

When teachers were invited to ask the accountant to deduct 10% of their salaries as their tithe to the church, he was the first to agree. Sadly, when he was repairing his corrugated zinc roof it collapsed under him and he was badly cut. With hospital treatment expensive and hard to get he did not go immediately for a tetanus injection and a few days later he died. There were no close relatives wanting to take responsibility for Sam and his sister Garmai, so they were found places in our hostels.

Three other members joined the hostel from Ghana where they had been looked after by The Salvation Army. At the start of the war many people, including young people with no known relatives, fled to Ghana, where they wandered around in gangs making nuisances of themselves. A dozen or so of these children were collected by Salvation Army nurses from Begoro Clinic. The boys were then housed in the clinic grounds and went to the local school. Some of them gave the nurses a hard time but gradually most of them developed into decent teenagers.

Philip Tapleh was the first of these boys to arrive back in Liberia to be reunited with his parents. Sadly, shortly before he got home his father died and there had been confusion between his mother and other family members. He had to stay with an aunt but felt he was a burden and not wanted. Seeing the state he was in, I let him join the hostel boys. Soon afterwards his friend Togbah arrived from Ghana and was also accepted into the hostel. He was the boy who later became the driver for the medical team.

Mark Blama was third and youngest of the group from Ghana. He had run away from the Army's care in Ghana and was found living with Ghanaian fishermen in a very dangerous part of town. It seems that while in Ghana he had learned Twi, the most common of the Ghanaian indigenous languages. I was told by Ghanaians that he could speak it as if he had been born in Ghana. We later discovered where his mother was living and sent him back to her but she had remarried and sadly didn't want to have anything to do with him. He had travelled for over an hour to meet with her but was not even offered a meal by his mother and step-father. We felt sad for him. He developed some fine musical talents and, as well as playing euphonium in the command band, also taught himself keyboard skills, eventually becoming leader of the command massed songster brigade. Funds were found for him to have some tuition on the piano. Seeing the potential in him a sponsorship was arranged to help him go to Norway. It was initially intended for him to stay for nine months to improve his piano playing, as well as study theology and learn about Norwegian culture.

Sadly, from The Salvation Army's point of view, while there he claimed refugee status and did not return. It is to be hoped that he will continue to develop his natural musical talent and one day return to teach others in Liberia. It has to be said that he was always inclined to be a bit of a maverick. Not only did he run away from the clinic twice, he also separated from the hostel boys during the 1996 troubles and finished up spending almost a year in St. Pedro in the Ivory Coast. The Red Cross had eventually brought him back to us, a little thinner, but in good health.

When the Command Mission Team was evangelising around Salala they came in contact with a young man called Varney. He was a singer and dancer at various places of entertainment in small towns around Monrovia. When he claimed Christ as his Lord and Saviour it was a major step, for he was a Muslim and his father was active at the mosque. When he went home and told his father that he had become a Christian his father threw him out of the family home and told him he would no longer pay his school fees. The mission team members went to remonstrate with the father but he wouldn't listen to them. When the father discovered that fees had been found for the lad he went to the school and ordered them to expel him. We then felt we had little choice but to admit him into the boys' hostel, where he would receive both protection and education in a Christian environment.

As I have explained, the boys' hostel had initially been started to accommodate former child soldiers but it did gradually accept boys like Varney as well as the increasing number of homeless destitute boys who otherwise had no honest means of supporting themselves. Many of the boys, and not just the former combatants, had been living lives that left much to be desired but very quickly some quite dramatic changes took place in their lives as they gave their hearts to the Lord.

I am encouraged because many of these young men are still active in church life as well as going on to get degrees and other qualifications which before coming contact with the Salvation Army they would have stood little or no chance of attaining. As I write, the last hostel boy is about to complete his senior high school studies and a significant chapter of the early history of The Salvation Army's work in Liberia will draw to an end.

Girls' Hostel

The opening of the boys' hostel had almost been forced upon us when boy soldiers, like Samuel Morgan, found the Lord while he was interned. Those boys had come from outside of Monrovia and it was not safe for them to return to their homes.

Above:
Flags waiting to be presented inside the church following a March of Witness at Congress celebrations.

Below:
Preparing for a Congress March of Witness around Paynesville

Top left: Gbarnga Church **Top right:** Opening of Kakata Church
Above: Monrova City Church with Major Nygård and friends.

Below: Paynesville Church / William Booth School Auditorium

Above:
William Booth High School with central quadrangle around the basketball court.

Below: William Booth Primary School situated on a terrace above the High School

Above:
New Len Millar High School from the front.
Old Len Millar School with Cols. William & Eleanor Norris.

Below:
The new Len Millar High School from the side entrance.

Above: Jackson Towah with Lt. Col. Brian J. Knightley & Prince Padmore

Above:
Abednego Morris and hostel boys

Below:
Oral Guanuc and Samuel Morgan

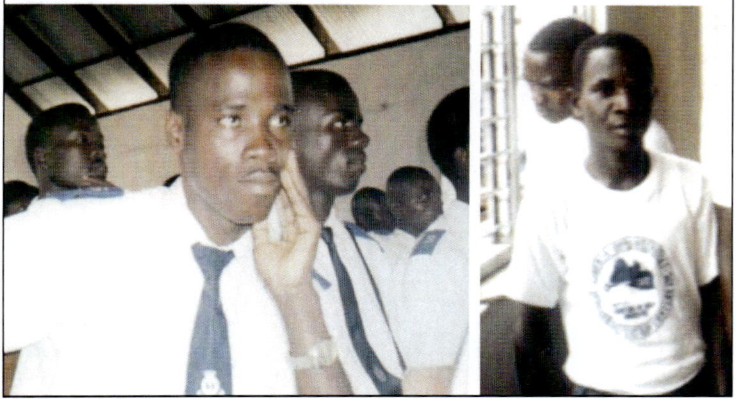

Above:
Girls' Hostel members on their way to Len Millar School with the school bus

Below:
Girls' Hostel members with their timbrels

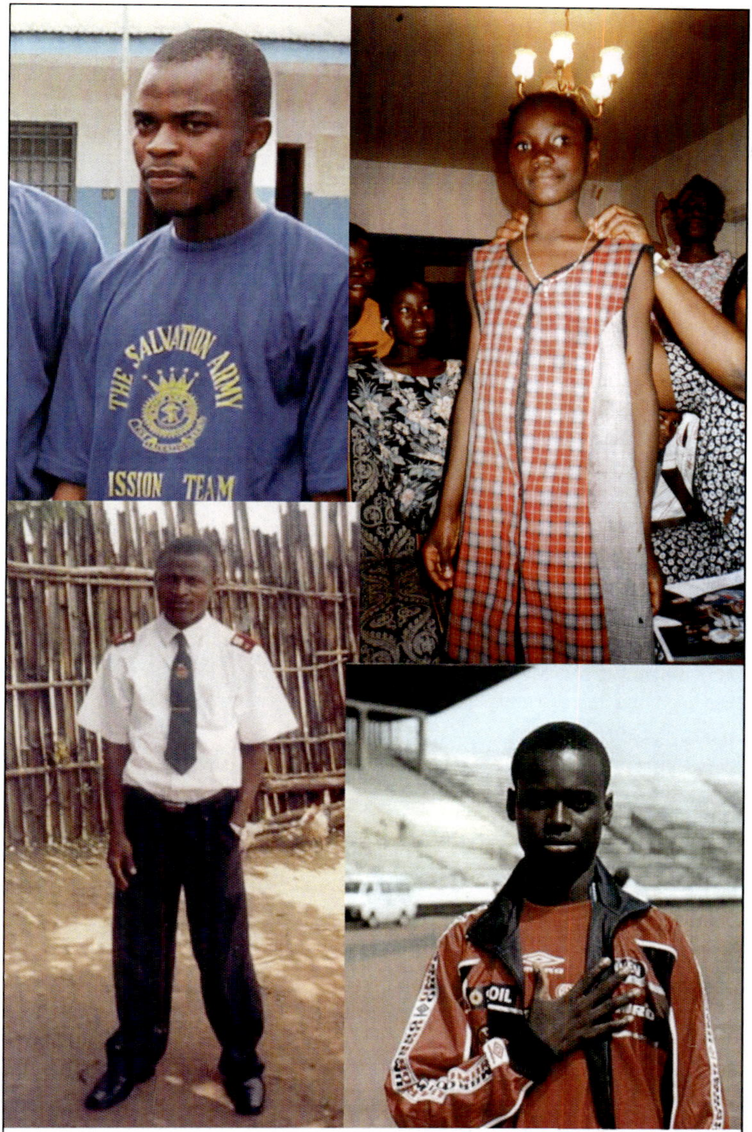

Clockwise:
Varney Sambullah, Nuku, Lt. Dennis Krah and Emmanuel David

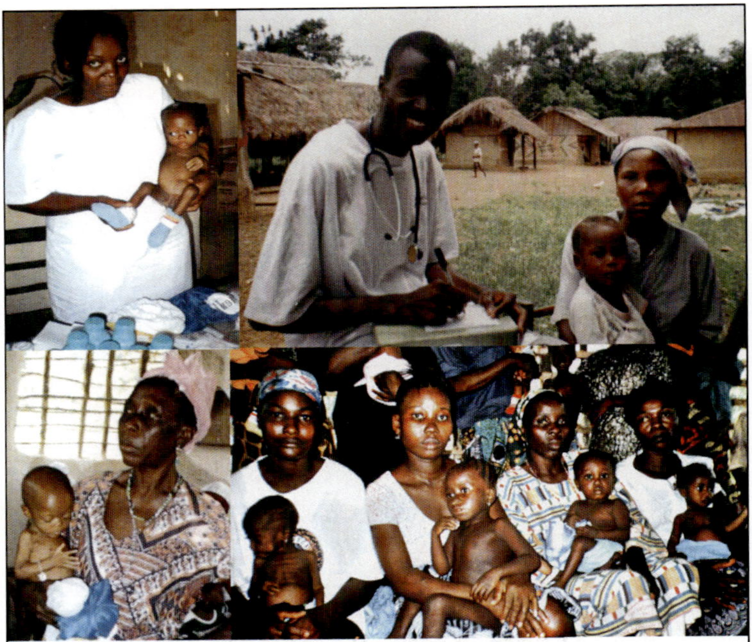

Above:
Left to right – Nurse Martha Natt & P.A. Mark; Mothers with babies at Menigay Feeding Programme Centre

Below:
Driver Togbah Karoch (former hoslet boy) with Mobile Clinic

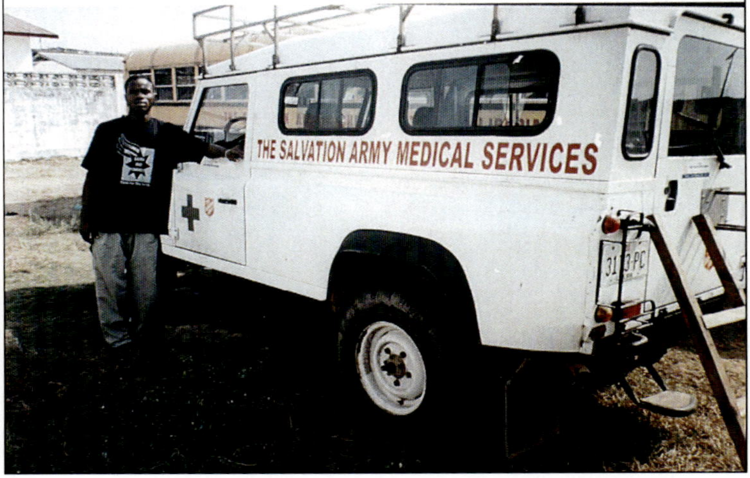

Above:
Typical example of a first corps (church) in a rural setting

Above:
A Church specially for Young People at Zwedru

Right:
Mr. Bainda walking in Liberia's forests.

Above:
Pump and Well supplied by the Salvation Army at Menigay

Below:
Command Mission Team with jeep and scary bridges for them to cross.

Above:
Women's Ministry dusplay their work – Tie-dying

Below:
Making progress with women's literacy classes

Above: William Booth Typing Institute

Above:
Monrovia City Church's 'League of Mercy' team taking food and water to prisoners in Monrovia's Central Police Station Jails.

Below:
Pioneer of Zwedru Corps – Shad Joloc (now Captain) with his wife and child.

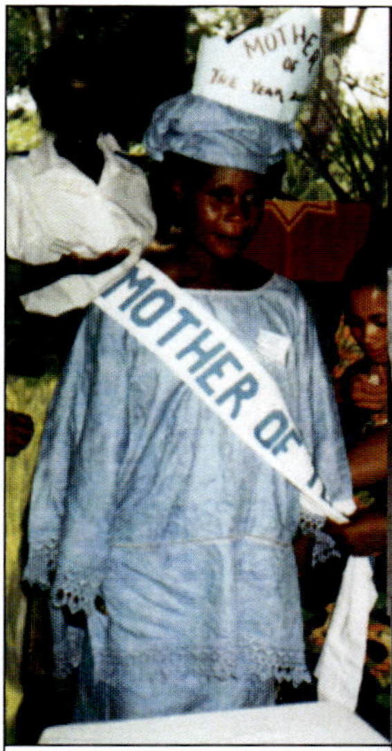

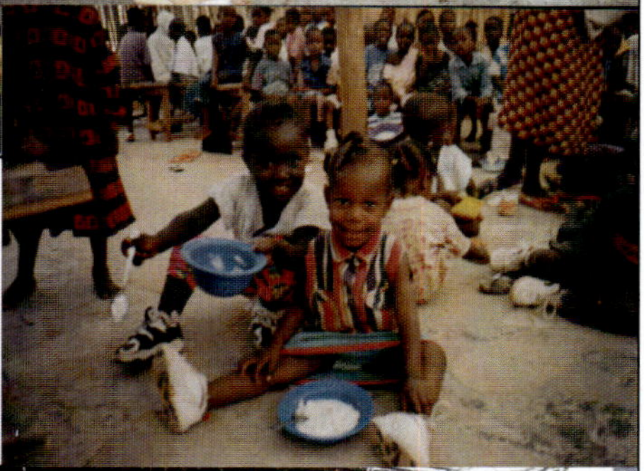

Left to right:
Mother of the Year, Dorothy, cooking in the early days; Hapy children at Gbarnga Day Care; and the land and building which took six years to possess.

Above: Bassa's winning Mission Team
Left: Playing carols in city at 33°C

Below: Digging a well at Salala for the officer's quarters with elderly displaced persons collecting food from the corps in the background

Left to right:
Future Liberian doctors? Jonathan Hart, Emmanuel Urey and John Dogba.

Below: Liberia Command Band.

Above:
Ernest Knightley – 2004

Above:
Ernest Ross – 1991

Below left: Lt. Cols Brian & Dorothy Knightley honoured by being presented with the Order of the Founder "*...for services over and above the call of duty...*"

Below right: Lt. Cols. Brian & Dorothy Knightley honoured by being 'Robed' according to the custom in Liberia.

There was not a similar problem with girls. However, as always in a fractured society like that found in Monrovia, young females were inevitably at risk of being exploited in some way. Nevertheless I hesitated to open a hostel for girls because I knew they would raise many more problems than boys, particularly when finance was likely to be a big issue. But, encouraged by our daughter, we decided to go ahead with a girls' hostel. The decision was that we would accept only girls who were at risk (mostly orphans) and had not yet reached puberty.

Some were accepted who were being brought up by aged grandparents and others, at the ages of only 8 or 9 years were involved in petty trading, selling cakes or water. Such children were often only allowed to eat once they had sold all that their guardians had given them to sell. They were vulnerable to abuse of all kinds as they wandered round the streets of Monrovia. Most had previously had little or no formal education.

When the first eight girls entered the hostel they seemed a sad group but very quickly they became happy and playful. They were much younger than the boys, who now became their big brothers. Many were, for the first time, sleeping on comfortable beds, eating adequately and having enough water to wash properly. On top of this, and probably the favourite for all of them, they were going to a proper school in full uniform with school bags containing pencils and copy books. To most of them this was a privilege which previously they could only have dreamed about.

As with the boys, most of them also needed some form of medical attention, the most common of which was for intestinal worms. After taking the necessary tablets the girls were horrified to see one of the girls with worms coming out of her nose and mouth.

She was a girl from the interior and her infestation was probably the worst. For other girls the worms left in a more common manner. Scabies, where mites get under the skin and cause sores and itching, was also widespread and took a long time to cure. Once the girls' health was sorted out they were then carefully monitored. This was possible because the matron in charge of them was, to begin with, Martha Natt, who we were sponsoring to become a qualified nurse.

When one of the girls, called Nuku, came to the hostel she seemed very withdrawn and solitary. Even the girls noticed, and drew Martha's attention to it. They also pointed out that she seemed to be hiding something under her pillow. On investigation it was discovered that she had a little muslin bag, tightly tied, in which was a variety of small objects. Martha recognised these as things used in the interior for witchcraft. Nuku had been born with one eye not in line with the other, giving her a strange look. This had encouraged her relatives to believe she had potential to become someone with magical powers. A relative had been preparing her to be able use these powers when she was a little older.

Martha called all the girls together and they made a bonfire onto which was emptied all the things from Nuku's little bag. She followed this with a brief talk on the power of Jesus to overcome all forms of evil and then had a time of prayer together. It wasn't long before Nuku was as boisterous and happy as the rest of the girls. By the time she was in her teens she had developed a beautiful singing voice which she used at school and in church.

Shortly after the opening of the girls' hostel I had a phone call from Norway; it was Major Inger Nygård to tell me that the Norwegian Salvation Army had been given a legacy that had to be used for the benefit of 'needy girls'. It was a large legacy and it was being offered to Liberia. We decided that it would be enough to buy the building alongside our Headquarters and would provide supporting funds for 30 girls for four years. This led to an increase in the facilities we were able to supply for the girls and for the numbers to be greatly increased.

When the building was finally adapted to meet the needs of the hostel it was our great joy to have Major Nygård present to cut the tape and declare the new hostel open. She was then the officer in charge of 'Projects' in Norway, and the one who had put forward the needs of our girls' hostel to Norway's Finance Board.

The new hostel had the added advantage of possessing a generator, so homework assignments and extra reading could easily be done in the evening. This gave the girls quite an advantage over many other students. Slowly many of the girls showed high academic ability, particularly those who had entered the hostel at a very young age. On leaving the hostel several chose to go on to higher education.

Sadly, when the four years of legacy money was all spent, financing the girls' hostel became increasingly difficult. The costs of keeping the girls in a hostel proved rather more expensive than providing for the boys. While we were the leaders of The Salvation Army in Liberia I managed, with increasing difficulty, to maintain the hostel but Major Dixon, the leader who followed me, decided that too many other needs were being sacrificed in order to keep the hostel open. The decision was then taken by him, and the leader who came after him, to phase out the girls' hostel. Relatives or foster mothers were sought to care for each of the girls with support being given for schooling, including a promise of further education, where suitable.

CHAPTER 11

INFAMOUS APRIL 6, 1996

April 6, 1996, is now written in the annals of Liberia's history. It was the time when the several warring factions had come together to form a joint administration.

Each of the groups, including NPFL (Charles Taylor's party), ULIMO J (Roosevelt Johnson's party) and ULIMO K (Alhaji Kromah's party), shared government ministries and Charles Taylor was the Chairman. All leaders were living in Monrovia and it was a very uneasy truce. Tensions were high and when a senior member of the NPFL was found dead on the beach near General Johnson's 18th Street base, repercussions were anticipated, though both of the other factions denied any responsibility for the murder. Taylor blamed ULIMO J.

The first sign of trouble to come was visible on the opening day of our 1996 congress celebrations. The Field Secretary from Ghana, Lt. Colonel Ofori, had arrived on the Wednesday, 20th March. On Friday, the first day of the congress, we woke to the sound of gunfire. Troops of the ULIMO J faction were running around outside our compound and surrounding streets. However, the action had been limited to our area and by 9 am things had quietened down. It had just been a show of strength.

After offering a prayer we left for the first of our scheduled congress services. By the next day, Saturday, the only battles going on were on the football field. We were even allowed to have a short, but impressive, march of witness.

By Sunday the Municipal City Hall was filled with almost five hundred Salvationists for the final service of the Congress which included, for the first time, an item by the newly-formed brass band. This was mostly made up from members of the boy's hostel and all taught by me.

Our guest for the celebrations, Colonel Ofori from Ghana, had to spend an extra two very tense and nervous days with us before he could return home because troop movements in the country had caused his scheduled flight to be cancelled. He would have been even more worried if he had known what mayhem was about to descend on Monrovia.

On Thursday, 4th April, people in 17th, 18th and 19th Streets were told by ULIMO soldiers that all movement in the area was to be restricted. However, being Good Friday, it was important for me to conduct the morning service at the City Church. By the time I returned from the service ULIMO troops had set up a position outside the gate of our compound and a road-block fifty yards up the road. For a moment I thought they might stop me getting back to the house where I had left Jackson and my wife but they didn't and I arrived back safely. Jackson then explained that during the night he had shouted at the rebel soldiers as they established their position outside our gate because he thought they were looters. Their response was to threaten to shoot him if they saw him again.

Feeling this made for a more tense time than necessary, I took some tea out to them and chatted with them. After I explained why Jackson had yelled at them they understood and he was also able to join us. The leader of the group was known as General War and the rest were all self-appointed colonels. We later discovered that General War was actually Captain Jabah in the AFL (national army). We were able to tell him about The Salvation Army and he promised to come to the church when the war was over. We didn't believe him but were later proved very wrong, for he eventually became a Salvation Army soldier.

Although having made peace with the men outside of our gates we still went to bed fearing that very soon something dreadful was likely to happen. Because of this I had left Ernest at the boys' hostel and invited Samuel (the former leader of the Boy Soldiers' Unit and now one of our hostel boys) to join me and Jackson at HQ. That evening the American missionaries, just up the road from us, left their house and went to sleep in the American Embassy. All the houses around us were now empty, with the residents having taken as many of their possessions as they could carry. Everything was eerily quiet; even the dogs seemed subdued. It was a very hot night, so Jackson and Samuel decided to sleep on the upstairs veranda.

At four o'clock the next morning; the sound was deafening. For a brief moment we thought it was the sudden breaking of a tropical storm. But this was no act of God. This was man at his worst. The war was on again, and this time it was starting outside our compound. There was beating on our door, with desperate cries for it to be opened. Like most people Dorothy and I are not at our best at 4 am and so it took a moment or two for the cacophony of sounds to make any sense. But within seconds I was dashing to the door to let Jackson and Samuel in whilst trying to put an item or two of clothing on – one never sleeps with much on at night in temperatures above 80°F. Being so close to the noise of rockets, mortars and heavy machine guns was an awesome experience, never to be forgotten. We knew that the corrugated asbestos roof would offer no protection from rockets and mortars, so we hurried downstairs in the belief that the concrete floor above the ground floor would provide a more effective defence.

The boys dived under the table and Dorothy and I sat in the cupboard under the stairs. Not for long though, as our four dogs insisted in joining us and then competed to be the one closest to Dorothy. It was a comical moment which even the boys saw the funny side of, and it did relieve the tension momentarily.

On Thursday of that week we had been surprised to find that our telephone line had been reconnected and was actually working. This proved to be a wonderful blessing during the next few days, for when the fighting was at its worse, we were actually able to contact family and friends in the UK to let them know that we were alive. It also enabled us to communicate with people in Liberia, and at one stage this included Charles Taylor himself. The phone had been off for weeks and we had almost given up hope of it ever working again. With no mobile phone companies operating in Liberia at this time, nor any internet services, a working telephone line was little less than a miracle in the position as we found ourselves.

Not long after we had descended the stairs a call came from Joseph Hage, Tony's brother, telling us that he was walking with his wife and baby-in-arms to Mamba Point Hotel. Rebels had already started to enter his house and were removing, at gun-point, just what they fancied. He asked for prayers as they made the perilous journey.

Moving out from the broom cupboard we crawled under the desk in the office, put a mattress on top, and simply waited. That mattress was later to fulfil a very useful role. At 9 am there was a pause in the firing. Naturally we were very interested to know what was happening outside but all that could be seen from our downstairs windows was the compound wall. We all crept up to the floor above to poke our heads just a fraction over the window sill. When we dared to look outside there was nobody in sight, not even General War and his men. We later learnt that the General had carried his leader, Roosevelt Johnson, from his base along the beach to the AFL barracks which became ULIMO's new centre of operations. There were houses on fire but not a human being in sight. Sporadic sounds of gunfire, mostly in the direction of the town, could be heard, plus, for a short time, the sound of a lone dog. That stopped suddenly following the sound of a rifle shot. We couldn't but wonder what was likely to be the fate of our four dogs.

After another three hours when not a soul had been seen from our window, Jackson and I risked walking up to the Boulevard. This was the main road, about 200 yards straight up from our compound. It was like walking on a stony beach. The surface of the road was covered in heavy calibre shells; evidence of the intense battle that had taken place during the early hours. The walls and gates of our compound were also peppered, clear signs that the firing had not been in one direction and we marvelled that nothing seemed to have penetrated our building. We saw some people in the far distance and some dead bodies lying in the road but other than that everything seemed strangely peaceful. When we returned to our quarters I told Dorothy that we had seen two dogs alive in the yard of the A.G. Missionaries and another at the home of our friend, Tony Hage, whose brother, Joseph, had fled during the night with his wife and new-born baby. Knowing my wife's love of animals I was not very surprised when she asked me to take some rice round to the dogs. The boys had cooked us some rice on their charcoal pot (we didn't dare put the generator on because it could draw attention to the fact that there were people in the compound). This second trip was a big mistake!

Whilst feeding the missionary's dogs we were hailed by an armed group who mistakenly we took to be the same ULIMO soldiers who the night before had been outside our gates. We gave them a friendly greeting, only to be ordered to stand still, while one of them put a knife to my chest and another stuck the point of his rifle into my back. They were looking for money but when they searched me they found nothing but they did take my watch (not a very expensive one). They then ordered us to take them to the house of Roosevelt Johnson. Jackson recognized some of them but wisely said nothing. If he had revealed that he knew them they would certainly have killed him and probably me too. As we headed toward Johnson's house they spotted a young Lebanese man and rushed off to grab him. We beat a very quick retreat back to our compound. It seemed to us that this man had appeared to save us, just as the sheep had in the story of Abraham and Isaac. Later we discovered that he was not harmed but actually joined the rebel group and some months later got deported by the new government.

Early on Easter Sunday morning the noise of rocket and gunfire gave way to an eerie silence except for an occasional shot or two in the distance. The four of us gathered around our dining-room table for prayer and a reading from the Bible. The verses selected were from Psalm 91 with its opening verse that spoke of security for those whose trust was in God.

"He who dwells in the shelter of the Most High will rest in the shadow of the Almighty."

This was a special time we have never forgotten because as we read through the whole Psalm it totally fitted our desperate needs of the moment. It brought great assurance to us that we would not be harmed and that we would receive divine protection.
"Surely he will save you from the fowler's snare and the deadly pestilence.
Under His wings you will find refuge.
You will not fear the terror by night or the arrow that flies by day.
He will call upon me and I will answer him;
I will be with him in trouble; I will deliver him and honour him." (NIV)

The psalm is full of such promises and as we read them and in prayer claimed them for ourselves a wonderful peace and calm seemed to fall upon us all. We felt sure that the worst was still to come but that we would all come safely through. Guns, knives and rockets would not destroy us – even the mosquitoes and lack of clean water would not bring disease upon us.

On Sunday, as any firing was coming from a long way away, Samuel slipped out to have a look around and to see if there was any way he could reach the Boys' hostel. He came back saying it would be risky because there was a rebel road block on the Boulevard. We were unaware at this time that the boys had long since fled to the Bushrod Island side of town, where it was quite a bit safer. He also reported that there were more dead bodies in the streets and that the rebels seemed to be making their way along the Avenue on a looting spree as they moved from house to house. Samuel thought that some of the bodies he saw might well have been where groups of fighters from the same faction had fought each other over looted goods.

As we had feared, the looters were heading in our direction. Unlike our quarters, those premises being looted which Samuel had seen had been vacated long before the rebels reached them. When the looters left they usually set the building on fire and we could see many burning, including the one belonging to the police chief. We knew it would not be long before they reached us!

Samuel had returned from his scouting trip with two guards who had appeared at the gate of the A.G. Missionaries as he passed their compound. They had been hiding ever since the firing had started and were nervous wrecks. They pleaded with Samuel to take them back with him to our compound which he did, but told them it would be up to me if they were allowed in. Naturally I could not refuse them sanctuary, though deep down I knew it could well be a short-lived haven that I was offering them. Sunday night was quiet but we still slept with our clothes on and tried to sleep down stairs under the table in the office.

On Monday morning heavy firing once again started in the city centre. After a short while a huge column of black smoke rose from the ground which glowed red. We correctly guessed it was a petrol station being blown up. The guns of the looters also seemed much closer so I attempted the impossible. Using a number that I had been given by a Lebanese friend some weeks previously. I phoned the NPFL leader, Charles Taylor. Much to my utter surprise and astonishment, not only did the phone still work but

I got right through to his office. I explained who I was and that I needed him to send some of his men to guard us and the Headquarters of The Salvation Army. The reply came that they would see what they could do and to our astonishment, one hour later, two of his men came to our gate and told us they were there to protect us and would need feeding. For a brief moment we believed that we were safe and could relax.

Sadly within a matter of just two or three hours these young men disappeared and the first of the rebels to hammer at our gates arrived not long after. He was a young man in his mid-twenties. He came driving a new sports car and carrying a hand-grenade. In the back of the car were two young boys (about twelve or thirteen year olds) who were manning a heavy calibre machine gun on top of the back seat. Our lads tried to avoid opening the gates but in the end the fighter threatened to blow the gates up and we could see from our balcony window that he was well able to do it. I then went down and opened the small pedestrian gate myself. The man had been demanding food and I wanted to dissuade him from actually coming into the building. By talking very calmly I managed to get him to believe that we had very little food in our compound (which was true). I pointed out that there was a good selection of food in the house from where the security guards had come. He accepted my reasoning but said that one of the security guards should show him the way.

Both of the guards were convinced that once they had pointed out the building the young boys would shoot him. As I could see that this was a real possibility, I told the man that 'I' would walk up the road in front of him and point out the house to him, which, without waiting for a reply, is what I did, half-expecting to be shot, and wondering if I would hear the sound of the gun before I felt the pain of the bullets.

When I got near I waited for the car to pull alongside me before I directed them to the right house. Thankfully, they hurried on to begin their looting. It was now clear events were beyond anyone's control and that the looting and killing would continue. Somehow we had to try to get away but this was difficult because the only hope of escape was the United States Embassy and the main area of fighting was between us and the embassy.

On Tuesday there was much more activity on the Avenues that ran horizontally across 17th Street where we were. We could see cars and pick-ups, some with their doors removed, travelling up and down fully loaded with looted goods. All we could do was to wait for the inevitable which, sure enough, at mid-day, arrived.

A truckload of armed men in their late teens or early twenties, drew up outside the compound and ordered us to open the gates. I went to speak to them, knowing that if I didn't they would simply blow off the locks and once they started using their guns they might not stop. My smooth words were not enough, neither was my warning that Charles Taylor had promised to protect us and keep us safe from fighters and looters. The leader, followed by most of his men, simply brushed me aside and went into the house. There were seven of them altogether and they were all armed. Apart from the one who was clearly the leader, they appeared to be country boys, not educated town people. At times they grabbed things, some of which they clearly had no idea what they were or what they were used for. At times they almost fought each other. This made us more nervous because bullets were likely to fly everywhere if they went out of control. Their leader was waving a pistol around as he climbed the stairs for a second time to grab more of our things so I politely and calmly asked him if he would stop waving it about because it might accidentally go off.

I should not have done that, for as I raised my hand he noticed I was wearing a wedding ring which he immediately demanded. At first I refused but when he put his pistol against my finger and threatened to blow it off, I handed it to him, grateful that it was one of those days when the heat had not swollen my finger. It came off quite easily and I was relieved that it was on my hand the ring had been spotted not Dorothy's because it always takes at least ten minutes and plenty of soap to remove hers. He was unlikely to have been that patient!

They took everything they could carry, especially all the HQ and personal electrical equipment, including word processors, amplifying equipment, radios, lamps, television and video machine. Then they filled up with all the smaller items and clothing from the bedrooms. Naturally they demanded all the cash we had, which in Liberian dollars was more than L$50,000 (about US$1,000). It was all neatly packed as we had just been getting the salaries ready to be stored until the end of April. This was because Dorothy and I were due to go on homeland furlough that week. As at that time the currency was all in L$5 notes, the cash filled three carrier bags. Naturally, this was one of the first things they grabbed.

Having this money was really quite fortunate because being in Liberian dollars it appeared formidable and so meant they did not push me too hard about any other possible cash that might be around. In the past, one expatriate couple had been shot dead because the fighters believed they were hiding US dollars somewhere.

When it had become obvious that we would have to let the fighters into the building Dorothy had quickly ushered all the dogs into the kitchen at the end of the house because she knew if the dogs ran at the intruders they would have been shot. The dogs seemed to feel the tension of the situation and even when the looters were moving around all over the house, they did not make a sound. Dorothy actually held onto the kitchen door handle and when one of the fighters went to enter the kitchen she told him that it was full of dogs and she just gave him a little peep inside and closed the door quickly to avoid both the dogs and the fighter from reacting. After that no one troubled her or the dogs.

They finally left when their pickup could hold no more. Dorothy and I marvelled at the fact that they had not found the new double cab pickup that we had in the garage, nor the Land Rover jeep that we had in the garden at the rear of the building. If they had noticed either of these we would most certainly have lost them. As we took stock of the situation we also realised that, with all the excitement, Jackson, Samuel and the two security men for the A.G. house had disappeared. At first we thought that they had been captured by the looters but I remembered having looked out of the window when they left and there was no room for them to have been carrying away four extra people. It was inconceivable that they had been shot because we would have heard any shooting in the compound. We looked in the building behind us as well as the field surrounding us; there was no sign of any of them.

It was not until thirty minutes later, when noises came from above us and one by one they lowered themselves through the flap in the ceiling that the puzzle was solved. Jackson had seen the fighters draw up outside and knew that as Liberians they would almost certainly be shot, whereas we expatriates, acting sensibly, were much less likely to be harmed because Charles Taylor never wanted international condemnation. Of course, not all of his men were too worried about such things or even knew of his wishes.

Once we were all together again we sat to decide what our next move should be. We guessed that we would now be subjected to a steady stream of looters and that some could be far more aggressive than the ones who had just left. With little left of any value in the building they would likely suspect we were hiding our valuables from them and so use some form of strong-arm tactics in an attempt to get us to reveal our hiding places. Jackson was sure that we would all be killed if we stayed in the building and urged us to attempt a breakout from the compound.

At this point Samuel volunteered to try to reach the small contingent of Ghanaian soldiers (peace keepers) who had established a base in 15th Street, just half a mile away on the other side of the main road. He had been a fighter himself, and was the most likely to survive if spotted moving around on the streets. We knew this would involve crossing the main road not far from a rebel road-block where we had seen people had already been shot, so were not sure that this was a good idea. As he insisted and it was the best chance for us all, I wrote a note for him to give the officer-in-charge, together with a photograph of myself. He then left after a brief time of prayer.

We wondered if we would ever see Samuel again; but at that moment the Lord brought back to our minds some of those verses from Psalm 91 that we had read together on Easter morning, and once again we claimed them in prayer on behalf of Samuel. We who remained thought it best to get ready and, with the hope that we might yet still save our vehicles, we put the batteries back into the vehicles. Next, things that were thought might be useful, like water, rice, beans and tins of meat, were thrown on the back of the pickup. Then began the job of pumping up the tyres of the jeep and pickup. A sufficient amount of air was pumped into the pickup's tyres for it to be driven but those of the jeep proved a much more formidable task. The little foot pump we had was no match for those large, thick and heavy tyres. The two security guards were in such a traumatised state they could do nothing to help but Jackson got busy immediately. It took almost 40 minutes to get one of the jeep tyres hard enough to drive on but just as we had started on the second there was banging on the gates. Slowly and silently we went back into the house and climbed the stairs so that we could peep out of a window to see who it was. To our amazement and immense relief we saw it was another hostel boy, also a former child soldier, Oral Guanue.

When the shooting had started he had escaped to St. Paul Bridge, the other side of town where it was relatively safe, along with the other hostel boys. He was worried about Dorothy and me so he had walked the six miles through the rebel lines to reach us. Not only were we happy to welcome him but he also assured us that many other Salvationists, as well as the hostel boys, had found safe refuge at St. Paul Bridge. It was he who, seeing our problem with the tyres, pointed out that we had a fully inflated tyre on the bonnet of the jeep which would need no pumping and could easily be changed with the one we were struggling with. Just as we completed the job we heard the noise of a large vehicle coming down our street and soon the top of a Ghanaian molem (large armoured vehicle) could be seen above our gates – Samuel had done it! Hallelujah!

Our rescuers were now outside the compound. The sense of relief and joy was quickly put to one side as I hurriedly asked the driver if we could take our vehicles with us. They said we should drive in front of their molem. Dorothy quickly got the dogs into the jeep and the boys piled everything available on to the back of the pickup. This included a cycle and the double mattress. I led the way in the pickup; Jackson followed in the jeep and the molem drove in the rear. When we got to the Boulevard I drove straight across it in order to get away from any visual contact with the fighters manning a check point just two blocks away and the jeep followed me. The molem, however, headed straight for the road block before taking a sharp right turn. I immediately had to swing round and we were now behind the molem rather than in front of it. I think we surprised the fighters who were blocking the main road as they stood cradling their guns.

It was an extremely scary moment, when just for a fraction of a second my eyes met one of those holding a machine gun. Only after we had passed them did they think to shout at us to stop. Naturally we just put our foot down and got to the base as quickly as we could. The fighters did follow us and tried to get the soldiers to hand over our vehicles to them but they dared not steal them from inside the ECOMOG base even though it was just a three-storey building with a checkpoint at each end of the road.

As soon as we reached the base the four Liberians mixed in with the other two or three thousand people who had fled there for protection. We were led to a three-storey building where we met some other expatriates who had been stranded when the fighting started. This included an Australian couple; the man was the head of the Lutheran World Services in Liberia and his wife worked for the UN. Together, with an Asian couple, they had been ordered out at gunpoint from the compound, where they worked and lived. Once their driver had handed over all the keys to their vehicles, he was shot dead in front of the expatriate workers. The mission head's wife had her dress torn off to see if she was hiding any jewels or cash. Whilst doing this they also smashed her spectacles. As you can imagine, when we arrived she was still in a state of shock.

There was also a family from the Philippines, a married couple with their two teenaged sons, who worked for World Vision and an American lady from the Lutheran Church was also there. She was quite well known to us as she had been in Liberia for many years. She had been in charge of the social side of her church affairs and had provided sponsorship money for many young people in Liberia, including some Salvationists. One other expatriate with us was a Belgium man who had only come to Liberia for the Easter holidays, but unfortunately he got rather more of an experience than he had anticipated.

All of us had arrived with just the clothes we stood up in; we were slightly better off than some because we had our own shoes but most of the others simply wore flip-flops. At night we were doubly blessed by having that mattress which Jackson had flung onto the back of the pickup. Without that, we would have had no choice but to sleep on the concrete floor.

Water was in very short supply, but for the added reason that toilet facilities were horrendous, we tried to drink very little. A cup of water was all that was available for a daily wash. We all pooled our food supplies which led to several strange meals but at least we did not starve. We had brought tins of beef and some milk powder plus one other special item – Dorothy's birthday cake. She had cooked it in preparation for her 62nd birthday, just a few days before we arrived at the base!

Soon after we got to the ECOMOG base it became clear that we would need more food. The Liberians down stairs, some with young children, were also very hungry. The Australian suggested to the Ghanaian Captain that if the molem could go back to his compound there might still be some rice in the store that could be collected. When they returned, bringing a few sacks of rice, I suggested that they could go to The Salvation Army's compound where, if the store room had not been completely looted, there would be boxes full of milk powder. When they agreed to go, I asked for Jackson to be allowed to go with them to show them where the milk was stored.

At the same time, I informed Jackson where I had hidden US$6,500.00 cash. I had stuffed it into the air vent of the drying machine but had told no one about this. Even my wife thought all the money had been looted. I had reasoned that if no one knew there was any cash left and had to face questioning, they would be convincing when they said all the money had already been taken. Now I was putting Jackson to the test. It would be easy for him to report back that the money had gone whilst hiding it somewhere for himself. I waited, praying that he would not give into any temptation to run off with it. Much to my relief, he returned with every dollar and the molem full of cartons of milk powder. He was quite badly cut because, not wanting the armoured vehicle to knock down the gates, he had entered over the wall which was covered in broken glass. The milk was invaluable because there were many displaced breast-feeding mothers and young children at the base.

It was clear to us that as expatriates we were a liability to the Ghanaian peacekeepers. Many uncomplimentary things had been said about the ECOMOG forces, and much of it may well be true, but those playing host to us were courageous and showed great skill in handling the rebels who often came taunting them. Even though we were clearly putting our guards under increased risk of attack, they never once showed any resentment towards us and were always polite and helpful. They had to go out on patrol from time to time and the base was sometimes left with just a handful of soldiers to man the roadblocks at both ends of the road as well as the buildings between them. If the gangs of rebels had chosen to, they could easily have overwhelmed the guards and killed the lot of us. Sometimes shots were fired at the building in which we were all staying. On one occasion I was foolish enough to stand on the third floor balcony where we were housed and heard the sound of a rifle shot as it passed by my ear and hit the stonework behind me. I never stood out on the balcony again!

Of course we were not only concerned about our own safety but also knew that our families and friends would be worried about us. The captain had radioed to the American Embassy to inform them that they had an American citizen, plus fifteen other non-Liberian nationals at his base and passed on all of our names. We hoped that this would have meant that our loved ones might have been informed somehow, that we were alive. We later found out that nothing was passed on, as everyone was engaged with problems nearer to hand.

Eventually, on Saturday, 13th April, the captain decided that we could be transferred to the ECOMOG headquarters in the former Coast Guards compound on Bushrod Island. It was impossible to get there by the short route over the New Bridge in the centre of Monrovia, so we had to go the long way round passing through Paynesville and Gardnersville. These were districts that were now occupied by rebels; each carrying a gun. As the vehicle passed through them the soldier with a machine gun on the turret held his gun at the ready all the time. The captain had told us we could only take one small case each, as the vehicle was very cramped inside. I took my laptop because I had just completed the designs and budget details for the new William Booth School. To me it was more important than anything else, though later we were to think that a little additional clothing would have been appreciated. I left keys to our vehicles with the Ghanaian captain and gave him permission to use them if he had an urgent need for them. I had to face the possibility that his unit could be called back to base.

I called Jackson to me and informed him that we were leaving. I knew that once the fighting ceased and people began to move around and return home, food prices would have gone through the roof. So I gave him US$1,000 dollars for him to give something to each of The Salvation Army officers with whom he came in contact and something for the hostel boys and himself. Oral had told us they were fairly safe for the time being at St Paul Bridge.

Most of the expatriates in our group were also penniless so they borrowed money from me too; all of which, I am grateful to say, was returned one way or other to The Salvation Army in later months. I also left a note giving Jackson and the hostel dean, William Johnson, permission to drive the vehicles if and when necessary. I gave the Property Manager, David Cooper, authority over all property matters and Lieutenant Gaymo oversight for the needs of churches and officers. This was all scribbled on a tiny piece of paper torn from my diary. I was later to find out that Jackson had his own adventures over the next few weeks but I was happy to learn that all the money was safely delivered and that no officer or hostel boy was killed or injured during this period of hostilities.

Arriving at the ECOMOG headquarters, we found it had become a refuge for many of the Liberian politicians, particularly those who had opposed Charles Taylor. Many were in a very disturbed state and clearly any sleep they had managed had been in their clothes. Usually Liberian politicians were overdressed in their suits and ties; here, the sweat and dust of the past week made them look very ordinary. These once feared 'big men', as they were known, were now reduced to a state where one almost felt sorry for them. I say 'almost' because it is not possible to forget that the county's present troubles were, in part, brought about these 'honourable' gentlemen's greed and selfishness.

It wasn't long before a message was passed to us saying that a vehicle was being sent from the American Embassy to collect the lady who was an American citizen. When it arrived, a typically large people carrier, two tough looking men in black body armour and a rather slight woman, got out of it. They each had guns in hip-holsters and the woman was in charge. At first they showed no interest in the rest of us. They only spoke to us when the American lady said she would not go with them if they did not take us all. We were then quickly told that all the men should take the UN pickup that was parked nearby, for which they had the keys. Most of the women and children were told they could climb into the American's MPV, though Dorothy was seated in the front of the UN pickup.

I was one of those who had to sit at the rear of the pickup and it was quite scary as we drove the short distance to the port. The streets were filled with people, almost all of whom were carrying some kind of firearm; this included some quite small children. We had been given a card with a print of an American flag on it to put on the pickup's windscreen. It was with great relief we saw what power was contained in that symbol.

Before we left the base I didn't know we were going to the port, but it had clearly been pre-arranged for us to go there. Waiting there were four ten-ton trucks and in the warehouses were sacks of rice and corn meal. We all helped to load the trucks, though I was not a great help because for the one and only time during the whole of this emergency, my asthma slowed me down. Once the trucks were full they drove off carrying one or two of us with them. I was put into the last of the vehicles and had to sit huddled in the space behind the driver. The tough American female security officer from the embassy was also in the truck sitting alongside the driver and just as we drove off I heard her pass on to the driver a message that she had just received over her hand radio. She told him there was a lot of shooting going on outside of the embassy at present, so they should be careful.

As we got to the foot of Mamba Point the deficiencies of the lorry began to show and we doubted at one point if it would be able to climb the hill. As it crawled up the slope, the smell of the dead bodies that lay all around was nauseating. All around were trigger-happy fighters, chasing each other in hijacked cars that they had painted with all manner of fearful designs and imagery. As we approached a rebel road-block halfway up the hill I dreaded having to stop because I doubted whether our vehicle would be able to start again. Our cargo would then have attracted the attention of everyone. Once again, I had to marvel at the power of that little card in our window. We were waved on and as the truck stuttered forward we tried to avoid as much eye contact as possible.

It was only later that we understood the importance of the food we were transporting. In a compound on the slopes opposite the embassy there were more than 15,000 displaced Liberians, all at the point of starvation. When we eventually drove into the US Embassy compound, we again thanked the Lord for his providential care. Months later the woman American security guard was deservedly decorated for her bravery during this crisis time.

Dorothy had arrived at the embassy a long time before I did and the other trucks followed her in quick succession. Our truck did eventually reach the embassy but not before the long delay had given Dorothy some anxious moments.

Once in the embassy grounds, we found everything was very well organised. We were documented, interviewed by a doctor and given bottles of water along with emergency rations. They took down the name of our organisation and asked who should be contacted to pass on the news that we were alive and well, but it transpired that this was not followed up.

Three hours later we were called to stand in line to be evacuated by helicopter. We were very impressed with the way the fully armed, no-nonsense marines carried out the departure procedures. Dorothy and I were almost the last of our batch to get into the helicopter and she was the final one sitting on her side of the helicopter. As the back was completely open to allow for a marine and his machine gun to be positioned at the rear, I was concerned for her as she suffers quite badly from a fear of heights. But miraculously, she was not troubled at all. She was even able to be interested in the forests, swamps and villages over which we were flying.

We were sad at leaving Liberia but knew we would return one day. When that would be, in a long time or short, we didn't know but we were determined to return to continue the work to which we had been called. We also left with nothing but admiration for the American military's bravery, efficiency, and courtesy as they dealt day after day with the influx of people into their embassy, most of whom needed to be transported almost immediately by helicopter out of Liberia.

By the time we reached Freetown it was getting dark. Normally this would have been the journey's end for British personnel because Sierra Leone has a British Embassy. However, Sierra Leone was now overflowing with refugees from Liberia so we were transferred straight away to a small military plane. After about two hours we landed and told we were now at Dakar, Senegal. Following registration, we were given water and told to wait for a representative from the British Embassy to meet with us.

It was almost midnight when our lady from the embassy arrived to deal with us. All those who had arrived with us had long gone and we had begun to think we had been forgotten. We were driven to a hotel and that night slept in a proper bed; the first time for a week. The next day we had a continental breakfast and as we left the dining room, much to our surprise and pleasure, we met our friend, Father Lee accompanied by Father Seckie (both now dead by natural causes), stepping out of the lift. Father Lee had his own tale to tell how he escaped a near-death situation. After sharing our adventures with each other, Dorothy and I walked out to see if we could buy something warm to wear. Dorothy was still just wearing her white blouse, the only clothes we had escaped with, and there was a cool wind blowing. It was Sunday and there was very little choice, so she bought a simple African gown that would go over everything she had on.

As we made our way back to the hotel we met a couple who were also refugees, staying at our hotel. They shared with us the news that a travel agent had agreed to open up his shop for them to buy a plane ticket. We decided to tag along with them and were fortunate to be allowed to book a flight back to the UK via Paris. This was only possible because we had the cash that Jackson had recovered for us. There had been just two seats left on Monday's flight to Paris.

As soon as we got back to the hotel I tried to contact someone at our International Headquarters but I had forgotten it was Sunday and only the night watchman was available. He agreed to pass on the message that "Major and Mrs. Knightley will be returning to Heathrow Airport" and I also gave him the flight number.

Once we arrived back in England we discovered the message I had left with the night watchman had been slightly misquoted in a way that caused our family some distress. They had been told "Major Mrs. Knightley will be returning…". Such a simple error, but it left our family and leaders fearing the worse. They knew Dorothy would never have returned without me if I was alive.

In the early hours of Monday morning we arrived at Dakar's International Airport only to find I had not been given all the ticket buffs; one page was missing. For a moment it felt as if the man at the ticket desk was going to refuse to let us on the flight. But after a half-an-hour and a time of prayer, word came back from the ticket supervisor that we could board the flight. It was a cold April day in Paris and we were shivering. The sun shining through the large glass viewing windows did offer some consolation. Much to our chagrin we found the flight to London was over-booked and that we had to be put on stand-by. Once again we had no choice but to pray and wait patiently. There was another flight to London that day, but we were hoping and praying that someone would have got our message and be waiting for us at Heathrow. If we did not arrive according to my message our family would have no idea where or when we would be coming. To our great relief our names were called and we boarded the plane on the last lap of our journey home. In spite of, or perhaps partly because of the faulty message, when we got to London, to our great joy we were met by our daughter, both our sons and their wives, and six of our grandchildren. Without us being able to inform them of our most urgent need on that cold April morning, they presented us with thick quilted jackets. To us that was an act of practical prevenient grace! With them was Major Pagett from THQ and Colonels Ted and Eva Cotterill. Apart from the Army's laptop computer we had lost everything, but we were alive and surprisingly healthy!

As we stood together and thanked God for our safe return, we also prayed for all those we had left back in Liberia whose survival was so dear to us. Even before we left the airport, we made it clear to our family and Major Pagett that we must return to Liberia as soon as conditions permitted. Neither our leaders, nor any of our family, questioned our position; they knew we were determined!

Now we were back in the UK we had time to think about those

we had left behind and wonder if they were safe. I knew Jackson would move out as soon as he thought it safe, in order to give help to the officers and boys. Samuel had already moved out before we left. He went to the building we were preparing for the girls' hostel. Lawson, the accountant, had stayed in that small compound and so Samuel took the dogs there because the Ghanaian soldiers had said that they didn't want them on the base as they could cause confusion. We later found out that Samuel secretly returned to our headquarters building to collect any food still there, including collect the tins of dog food. On one of his trips he was stopped by a fighter and told to hand over the tins he was carrying. As the fighter could not read the label on the tin Samuel told him that it was 'dog food'. With a picture of a dog on the tin the rebel took this to mean it was the meat of a dog. Samuel said the young man seemed to enjoy eating it. Sadly, it is true that many Liberians do eat dog meat and two of our dogs were shot by fighters for meat. The two eldest dogs, Petra and Sheba, were cared for by Samuel and when we returned we found them in Mr. Hage's yard, emasculated but alive.

We learned later, that a day or two after we had been evacuated, Jackson set out to make his way over to Bushrod Island where he understood from Oral that he was likely to find the hostel boys. He also expected to find some of the officers there. Before he reached Paynesville, however, he was captured by some of Taylor's fighters, who took him to the NPFL compound. There he was stripped of most of his clothes and made to sit on the ground with a lot of other young men. After a while an NPFL officer came looking at the captives. As he passed by Jackson he turned to have another look and then realised who it was.

Years before, the young boy Jackson had lived for a time on a

Baptist Church compound where he carried out small duties. The NPFL officer had also worked there and now recognised Jackson. He immediately ordered someone to recover Jackson's clothes for him and took him off to the place where he was staying. They chatted for some time and then a full bowl of rice was set before him covered with chunks of meat. Jackson was extremely hungry but feared to touch any of the meat. Not because he believed it to be poisoned but because he didn't know what the meat was. For days there had not been any meat to be found and yet here was meat in abundance. It could of course have been looted from the supermarket but that had long ago been cleaned out. His great fear was that the meat could have been human flesh, so he politely refused saying he was not hungry. As soon as it was diplomatic to do so he thanked the fighter for freeing him and set off again to meet up with the boys. He had not carried the cash with him on this trip because he wanted to find the boys first.

He found Ernest at the Bushrod Island Church and the boys were not far away. Once he knew where they were he talked with a ULIMO K fighter who had a pickup and persuaded him to take him back to the ECOMOG base, saying he wanted to collect some important papers and that he had something nice to give him if he would oblige. He got back to the jeep where he had hidden the cash and collected our canteen of cutlery as payment for the ride. The fighter was happy with his 'payment' and took Jackson back to Ernest.

The cash was shared out and then he, Ernest and the hostel boys all decided to buy tickets for the boat called *Bulk Challenge* which was in the port. As everyone tried to get on to the boat it began to list badly and some people decided it was going to sink and quickly disembarked. This included nearly all of the hostel boys.

Jackson and Ernest, however, remained on board and, unknown to them, so did hostel boy Mark Blama. The boat, grossly over loaded, set out from the port still listing. It was not a passenger boat and had little or no facilities for passengers. Most importantly, it had nowhere near enough water. In the tropical temperatures, the people suffered. To make matters worse, no country would let the boat dock for West Africa countries were already flooded with Liberian refugees. But this was cruel, and those on board began to believe that they would all die. When Christians prayed the Muslims joined with them; when the Muslims prayed, the Christians joined with them!

After more than a week at sea the boat was permitted to dock to permit women and children to disembark. Mark took hold of a woman's hand, not knowing who she was and posing as her son he was allowed to disembark from the boat at St. Pedro, Ivory Coast. The ship was then sent away from the Ivory Coast. The plight of those suffering on board the *Bulk Challenge* eventually became international news. Pressure was then put on the Ghanaian Government to have pity on the people on board and after more than a month of moving up and down the West African coast, the *Bulk Challenge* boat finally docked at Tema City, Ghana.

Pictures of people disembarking were shown in the UK on national television and we watched intently to see if we could spot Jackson or Ernest as word had reached us that they were on board. We didn't see them but I contacted The Salvation Army Headquarters in Ghana and asked them to keep a watch-out for these two young men. All the refugees were taken to a camp at Buduburam where there were already more than 20,000 Liberian refugees. Within a few days Jackson reached the Army in Accra, where Colonel Ofori welcomed him and supplied food and clothing for him and Ernest. He also helped him with money to get a taxi back to the camp.

The colonel then sent a message for me to be informed that Jackson and Ernest had been found and that they were well. With grateful thanks I replied, telling him that when we returned we would travel via Accra and I would pay for them to complete the journey by plane with us.

CHAPTER 12

RETURN TO LIBERIA

Back in Liberia, just prior to the dramatic events of April 6, 1996, we had been planning the Easter celebrations and at the same time getting things ready for our two-month furlough in England. Our slightly premature return home and the delay before re-entering Liberia only added just four weeks to our leave. We were away three months instead of two.

As soon as news reached me that planes were once again flying into Monrovia I made plans to get there as soon as possible. At first our friends in Ghana were still saying it was too soon and too dangerous but I appealed to the General, who agreed I could go but that initially I should go alone to prepare the way for my wife to join me. Not only was this a safety precaution but a sensible practical decision. Word had reached me that our quarters and home had been completely looted; not just the furniture and personal possessions but also the carpets, doors and window frames not to mention the generator and even the wires in the wall.

As soon as permission was granted I flew out to Accra where I collected Jackson and Ernest. I have to admit it; we were all in tears as we hugged each other. We had doubted that we would ever see each other again. In fact, each in our turn had moments when we had considered the possibility that the next time we would meet would be in Glory!

As the boys and I flew off from Accra toward Abidjan, where we had to exchange planes, my mind was dwelling on what we were going to find when we arrived. We had not been told of any deaths or casualties of Salvationist personnel but wondered if the worst news may have been kept from me until I arrived back. I was so absorbed in my own thoughts that when the plane landed and people began to alight I stood up and led the others off with me. It wasn't until we got to the exit barriers that I realised that we were not in Liberia but actually in Nigeria. I hadn't known that the flight we were on was heading east before it went west! All three of us ran as hard as we could and just managed to get back on the plane, feeling very silly but thankful that we didn't have to spend a day or two in Lagos. Ernest had been very fearful when the plane took off in Ghana because he had never flown before but he was too out of breath to worry about it the second time.

We arrived in Monrovia from Abidjan on Tuesday afternoon, July 9th, 1996. To our great delight we were met by the hostel boys, some local officers and soldiers, plus Tony Hage. While there was still a little daylight I walked down to the Headquarters' building with our home above it. Physically, it was just as Tony had explained it to me over the phone but when viewed first-hand it gave an air of utter desolation. Some doors were missing, others hung dangling off one hinge; papers were strewn all over the floor, made to look even worse because rain water had blown in through the spaces that had once contained large sliding windows. In the bathrooms even the commodes and sinks were missing. There was no furniture remaining, apart from two empty filing cabinets and half a cupboard. All crockery, cutlery and appliances (cooker, air conditioners and refrigerator) had gone along with the kitchen sink. The bedrooms were completely empty of furniture as well as pelmets, curtain rails and wiring for the lights.

In the yard the grass was now waist high, adding to the appearance of abandonment and the 5 KVA generator was gone along with the hand pump above the well. The looters had been ruthlessly efficient. As I walked back towards Tony's house where I would be staying, the property manager, David Bainda, probably sensing how I was feeling, told me that he and some of the boys had already located various items that had been looted. This included several doors and window frames, as well as one or two items of furniture.

Though they were clearly ours he still had to pay something to get them back. Sometimes an ECOMOG soldier could be persuaded to order an item to be returned but it was often easier and possibly cheaper (the ECOMOG soldier would still expect to get paid for his services), to haggle with the looter and pay up.

The band I had started had begun to take shape. It was based mostly on hostel boys, as I could more easily arrange to hold practices with them at a time convenient to my schedule. Sadly, their instruments too had nearly all been looted and it meant that once again the word had to go out that brass instruments were needed in Liberia. The appeal did not go unanswered and when in October the first container to arrive after our return it contained a real assortment of instruments. It is true that most of them were very old but the majority were able to be made playable, even if they did sometimes need a bit of string and tape to hold them together.

One very good Eb Bass turned up that was in excellent condition. I later found out that it had come to us by mistake and actually belonged to a bandsman at Wealdstone, UK. The officer of that corps had been too eager to support us! A few years later I did meet Brother Wiggins whose Eb Bass it was. By that time he was able to smile about it and to say he hoped it was being treated with the respect it deserved. Where the instruments went to I don't know as the AFL band was the only one operating at this time in Liberia. When the *Bulk Challenge* reached Ghana it was found to contain many looted items belong to aid-agencies, so who knows? They could have turned up in Ghana.

Samuel had gone back to HQ and rescued my cornet and kept it in the ceiling of the girls' hostel. One trombone, however, clearly came to an untimely end as I found its bell section being used as a funnel at a gas station.

During my first week back I was able to move around freely and visited officers in their quarters. It was a relief to discover that none of them had suffered any physical harm during the emergency and only one of them had suffered any significant loss of property. Lieutenant Wheiger had lost his bed and mattress but I was able to replace this quite quickly.

The only building of ours in Monrovia that had suffered any damage was the City Church, but this was minimal compared to many other buildings in the city. It had a few bullet holes in the main roof and a rocket had taken off some of the zinc at the corner above the platform. This rocket had gone on to make a hole in the roof of the auxiliary building which is now part of the quarters. About forty loose chairs had also gone missing. Fortunately, the church had opted for pews and these had been too heavy to be taken away. Once the most dangerous phase of the fighting had passed, Mr. Bainda, our property manager, had quickly arranged for a few people to sleep in the church and as a consequence most of the doors and windows remained intact and the pews were not carried off for firewood.

Close by, our typing school had been cleaned out. It lost thirty typewriters, two computers, thirty chairs and twenty small desks. In 1995, when we opened the typing and computer school, it was quite innovative. With very little electric current available, except with the assistance of a generator, manual typewriters were used in practically all businesses. Firms with generators could have the luxury of computers but only the wealthiest of the aid agencies could access the internet via their satellite communication facilities. Many of our typing graduates quickly found employment; some in quite high positions. It was really sad, therefore, that we had to close this school down until we could manage to bring some more typewriters into the country. We were able to restart it eventually when almost forty typewriters arrived in a container bringing a generator from the UK for Headquarters.

We had sent out an appeal to churches in England and Major Dennis Lomax, at the time leading the corps at Carlisle, shared this with his local newspaper. They made a feature of it and almost forty typewriters were handed in at his corps for us. The major then drove all the way down to our shipping agent at Gerrards Cross and just got them there in time to be shipped out to us with the generator. With this donation, supported by machines from several individual people, we were able eventually to start up a second typing school.

Of course, the hostel boys had been left without anything too. All their furniture was gone, as was all their pots and pans. The hostel was completely bare. I came with some funds, so was able to replace their mattresses for them though for a time they had to sleep with them on the floor.

Before leaving I had asked people for white shirts (for school and the church) and shoes, so I was able to supply each of them with at least two shirts and a pair of shoes. I was surprised to find them looking so well and lacking any noticeable signs of trauma. I guess they had grown up with danger most of their lives, so were able to take the stress of the past months in their stride. The camaraderie they had between themselves was also a factor for, apart from Mark Blama, all of the boys had stayed together as a group. I feel the Dean of the hostel at that time, William Johnson, has to take some credit for this as he didn't desert them.

On the first Saturday back I met all Headquarters' staff and gave each of them their wages for April and May. The teachers had only been contracted until the end of May so were not officially due to receive anything. However, with the urgent needs of their families in mind I gave them half a bag of rice each to keep them going until school started again in September. Each of the officer-couples was given a whole bag of rice together with their allowances up to the end of August.

It seems that during the whole of this recent war taking place in the centre of Monrovia there were only two Salvationists killed. A boy and his father from the City Corps died when a rocket hit the chapel in the barracks where they were sheltering. It also has to be recorded that three of our youths took some part and carried arms during the emergency and so had to be suspended. Happily, not one of the child soldiers who had been taken into the boys' hostel, returned to the fighting arena. Four members of the City Corps, which included the corps secretary and treasurer, had their homes completely destroyed during the fighting and had to live in a camp for displaced people for many weeks.

As I drove round the City I was shocked to see the devastation. Whole streets had been completely flattened, big churches burned-out and at least two large schools damaged beyond repair.

Petrol stations had been blown up, along with many cars and trucks. In the centre of the city tall buildings that had been part of the commercial structure of Monrovia were just skeletons with no roofs, no doors and no windows; not even window frames.

It was not just The Salvation Army Headquarters that had been completely looted. We ourselves had lost practically everything. On our departure from Liberia by American helicopter, all we took with us was a laptop and some documents. When I returned just three months later there was not a single item which belonged personally to us remaining, either in the building or at the ECOMOG base.

When we had first travelled to Liberia we had taken little more than what two suitcases would hold. But slowly, as containers were sent out with a variety of things for our Headquarters, many of our more personal possessions were slipped in. We had decided that for the time being Monrovia was our home and so the little things which make up a home which at first we had put in store, gradually began to grace our Liberia home. Now they were all gone. No clothes, no books, no items of personal furniture, no ornaments; all were gone. Somehow, as I have mentioned earlier, Samuel (who had been with us during the crisis time) had managed to rescue my cornet. One or two photographs lay together with a heap of dirty papers on the floor and one thing I was particularly happy to find in that same pile of rubbish was my Teacher's Certificate. It was necessary, while I was busy opening schools, to have evidence of some qualification. Back in England we had just one trunk of things in store.

In material terms, this was all we owned in the world which we could call ours. Though it may be difficult to believe, we hardly missed a thing. We had never been very worried about material possessions so it was not the kind of problem we would weep much over, though obviously some essentials had to be obtained. I am pleased to be able to say that all essentials were very quickly supplied at almost no financial cost to ourselves. One way or another, God saw to it that what we really needed, we received. He touched the hearts of so many kind people back home in the UK that our joy was overflowing with practical signs of love and caring from all directions.

It was with mixed feelings that I approached my first Sunday back. I felt sure that our members would have scattered and that even if they were still in Monrovia they would be more concerned with rebuilding their lives and homes than attending a service. So I went to the City Church expecting to find just a handful in the congregation, but was amazed to see almost a hundred and fifty people gathered; many in their uniforms. The singing was full-throated and the testimonies were heart-rending. Even the choir was there in some numbers. When I got up to speak I was almost overwhelmed with emotion. All of these people had faced near-death experiences but were cheerfully singing praises to God and voicing prayers of thanksgiving for deliverance. And they were all so cheerful! I was proud of them. I had thought I was returning to a people crushed by the fighting; an Army that would take years to rebuild, but I was facing a congregation raring to go forward. It was almost as if the testing time they had passed through had invigorated them. The call kept on resounding round the church; "God is Good – All the Time".

For the next two weeks my time was spent mostly trying to refit the Headquarters and make our quarters habitable. Some things that were needed I left for Dorothy to sort out when she returned but windows and doors were essentials as were the bathroom and kitchen fixtures. The Freeport was already busy bringing in ships to re-supply the city, so it was not as difficult as I had expected to obtain some items. Mr. Bainda was also kept busy searching the surrounding streets for our looted items and negotiating a price for their return. During this period I was able to stay with Tony Hage in his home. He was extremely helpful, generous and kind, and this hospitality was also extended to my wife when she returned a few weeks later.

When I left England to check up on conditions in Liberia following the events of April 6th, I booked my return tickets from Ghana in advance. To return there, however, I had to fly from Spriggs Payne Airport in Monrovia and, knowing the unreliability of the local airline, planned to take a flight that would get me to Ghana in good time. When that day came it started sunny and the boys from the hostel came to sing me off. By the time of the flight, however, a storm was about to break and it was announced that the rain had become too heavy for the plane to take off in Accra; so we should all return the next day. The next day the plane came but because the rain clouds were so low the pilot could not see the runway, so he returned to Abidjan without landing in Monrovia. On the third day the aircraft came and attempted to land but crashed in the swamp as it touched down! The city airport was not really meant for large planes but as the international airport was derelict it was the only option. Fortunately no one was seriously hurt but the runway was blocked and it was anybody's guess when it would be cleared. I now began to be concerned how I was going to get to Accra in time for my BA flight in two days time. It was then that Tony Hage made a suggestion to me that at first seemed horrific. A Lebanese friend had negotiated with a member of Taylor's militia, who had a jeep in the parking lot, to drive him to Liberia's border with the Ivory Coast. The suggestion was that I should go with them. But it would mean driving many hours through the interior of Liberia, which was under the control of rebel fighters. I had never been to these districts; it had never been safe enough. It was also well know that within the NPFL there were many factions, some of which were not terribly friendly to one another. But I just had to get back to London on time because there was no way at this stage of affairs to communicate with either my wife or headquarters to inform them of a change of plans.

I remembered how people had feared the worst when we were fleeing earlier in the year and I didn't want anyone, particularly my wife and family, to go through the same stresses again. So, full of apprehension, I agreed!

I had very little baggage but I was carrying over US$1,000 and didn't know where to hide it. I thought it was quite likely that we would be stopped and searched and I didn't want to lose it. We were made to stop several times and it seemed some negotiating took place but we were not harmed in any way. When my wife and I had first travelled to Liberia we had found the immigration officials at Abidjan had been very fussy when I had just wanted to go to the town and back without a visa for the Ivory Coast. I wondered, therefore, if we were in for a hard time now as we got closer to the border. I have to admit I anticipated a big problem. But first we had to get over the Liberian border.

We stopped at Ganta, which was clearly an important rebel base with a high-ranking fighter in charge. Our driver left us for what seemed like a life-time, though in reality it was only about twenty minutes. My Lebanese companion seemed very calm but we did not speak. Eventually the driver returned and without saying a word simply drove on. The next part of the road was very difficult to negotiate because the road at times was stony and at others, just like a swamp. After an hour my companion lent over to me and said we are just about to reach the Ivory Coast. Clearly he had been this way before. Then, almost immediately, there appeared a clearing in the forest through which we had been passing. Ahead of us was a small rickety bridge and beyond it a small building. I had imagined that the rough road we had just driven on was leading to some secret border crossing where there would be no police or officials waiting when we entered the Ivory Coast. I was wrong, for I could see both. We had to get out to show our documents which in my case were not complete. The questioning was in French, which compounded my difficulties. Fortunately the Lebanese man spoke French fluently and negotiated a price for our passage through.

It could have been a lot worse and I was greatly relieved when we were allowed to climb back into the jeep and proceed to Danane. Here the driver left us and it was only then that I discovered, to my great relief, that we had passed through all the checkpoints with relative ease. Our driver was on a special mission for Charles Taylor, about which we knew nothing.

We had been on the road for ten hours by the time we reached the Ivory Coast, so decided to eat at the one decent hotel in the town. When I had accepted the lift I did not have time to look at any maps of the route. In my ignorance I had thought it would be just a couple more hours before we reached Abidjan. But when we went out to charter a taxi I heard the taxi driver tell my Lebanese colleague it would take about eight hours. Later I discovered, much to my surprise and disappointment, that we were still almost four hundred miles from Abidjan. We left the hotel at about nine o'clock in the evening and it was very dark as soon as we left the town. I had thought that with such a long journey still to travel I would have a sleep. It was an utter impossibility. The driver was a mad-man!

In the pitch black he drove round corners as if he was on a race track and oncoming trucks, of which there were many, with headlights pointing at all angles, never slowed him down the least little bit. I know I joked about it afterwards but at the time it was as almost as nerve-racking as the time we waited for looters to reach us at our headquarters. I am not a good passenger at the best of times. Even in Liberia I mostly drove myself. From Danane to Abidjan, there was to be no sleeping for either me or my Lebanese companion. But after much prayer, we reached Abidjan – shaken but alive.

The taxi dropped us at the five-star Sofitel Hotel in Abidjan. Here my companion left me to go and stay with a relative. I went straight to the wash-room to get cleaned up, though I didn't have any change of clothes to put on. It felt better to be clean and it did wake me up.

Now I had to work out how to get to Accra in time to catch my BA flight to London. Once again God was on my side because the hotel had its own travel agency and I was able to book a flight to Accra that was to leave in four hours time. The hotel found me a taxi and I was at the airport in good time. I arrived in Accra with just six hours to go before my BA flight was due to take off. So, having a multiple entry visa for Ghana I slipped out, had a meal, and returned ready for the last lap of a very eventful and exciting journey home.

In retrospect it did seem like a miracle that I had managed to get back at the pre-arranged time. No one at the UK end had heard anything about the plane that crashed or my journey through rebel lines, so no one had been concerned or fretting about me. It was just one more of those never-to-be-forgotten experiences.

The next two weeks were spent collecting as many useful things as possible. It was planned for a container to be sent out in the second week of September. Its main cargo was to be one large generator for headquarters but our congregations all over the country had heard of our plight and had been asking us what we needed and where to send it. As space would be limited we sometimes had to turn down some things but stacking chairs, shoes, typewriters, sewing machines, white shirts and blouses, office supplies and equipment, brass instruments and Salvation Army Song Books, were stacked tightly into the container.

Fortunately our shipping agents were very kind and patient. As things arrived they stored them for us until the container was due to be shipped to Monrovia. I tried to let them know when goods were going to arrive but often didn't know myself. It made for some interesting surprises when the container was opened up in Monrovia! There were almost a hundred flight attendant light blue skirts and jackets from an airline. I have no idea how they came to be put into the container but they were all made good use of. Some things we had to collect ourselves but where possible we got the donors to drive them to UNIMATCO at Gerrards Cross.

Knowing that food was short, particularly the kind Dorothy could cook and I could eat, we did a lot of shopping for ourselves. This included things like tins of peas, carrots, beans, fish, meat pies, packets of powdered milk, custard powder, dried cooking fruit, powdered potatoes, cereal and flour. The food in tins was estimated to supplement our rations for about a year.

The less durable commodities were only sufficient for three months, as by that time the humidity, weevils or cockroaches would have destroyed them. We also took three weeks supply of dehydrated meals (soya mince etc.) in our cases, because the container was not due to arrive for at least three weeks and we knew all the shops had been stripped bare. Our favourite grocery shop had been burnt to the ground. Two of our dogs had survived so into the container went two cartons of tinned dog food along with two sacks of dry dog food. The dogs were our main security and we believed in treating them well.

We flew out of Gatwick Airport at midnight on Sunday, September 1st, 1996, happy to be returning to the country we now felt sure was the place and people to whom God had called us. In Ghana we stayed one night in the home of the Chief Secretary and the next flew on to Abidjan. There we spent the night in the airport hotel, which revived memories of our first journey to Liberia. On Tuesday afternoon we flew on to Monrovia. Once again we were met by the hostel boys, Jackson and Tony Hage. The customs tried to give us a hard time with my laptop and especially with the printer, which was in a carton. We finally convinced them, with the assistance of a friendly Ghanaian ECOMOG soldier, that they were for our use and not for resale. In the future we remembered never to try to take anything through customs in a carton. It is always worth putting everything into a suitcase, even if it means taking an extra case. Cartons always attract the attention of the custom officials. Once again Tony Hage assured us that we were both welcome to stay as long as necessary at his house and a meal was waiting for us as we reached his compound. The following day I took Dorothy to the headquarters building and to her great surprise and delight, after five months away from them, the dogs still remembered her and came running to greet her.

The same company of Ghanaian ECOMOG soldiers was still based in 15th/16th Street, where we had been for five days during the emergency of April 6th. Jackson and I had collected the vehicles when we had returned some weeks previously but the captain had not been around then, so we took time to see him and to thank him for the care and protection he had given us, particularly for sending his armoured vehicle to collect us from our headquarters when we really did fear for our lives. All of the soldiers had been very courteous and had put our needs before their own, so we took a little gift for the captain and each of his men. The captain told us he intended to retire on his return to Ghana and start a farm. We wished him every success.

When I returned to collect Dorothy, Mr. Bainda had got busy setting his workers the task to put the headquarters building and our quarters back into some kind of liveable condition. This included rewiring throughout the building, installation of the necessary electrical fittings and the two air-conditioners. Dorothy went off to purchase as many of the items she knew would not be coming in the awaited container. She was surprised to find that most of what was needed was available but shocked also at the prices being charged for them. It wasn't long before we wished we had put many more day-to-day items in the container! However, within a couple of weeks most of the essential items had been obtained; some new and some second-hand. Eventually the container did arrive, three weeks late, complete with the generator that would be important to the quality of our lives.

Tony Hage had given over his house to us for almost two months. I had dealt with the business of the Command in his home, including meeting many Salvationists who wanted to see me, and he never once made me feel we were being an imposition. He was both patient and gracious. He had been a wonderful host and our thanks were most sincere when we eventually were able to move into our transformed home and headquarters.

There had been no absolute winner in the fighting that had taken place in April but the NPFL (Taylor's faction) finished up being very dominant. Roosevelt Johnson's men were now mostly holed up in the city barracks and some nearby streets. Tensions were still great, and maverick groups from either side were still involved in various acts of lawlessness, inside and outside the city. One afternoon Jackson was driving our jeep in town when a group of ULIMO J fighters stopped him at gunpoint, ordered him out of the vehicle and demanded the keys. He had no choice but to give it to them and they drove off in the Land Rover which we had managed to keep throughout the most intense time of hostilities. It was beginning to get dark when this happened, so Jackson came back to headquarters determined to make an attempt to get it back in the morning. Early the next day he boldly went into the barracks and asked to speak to Captain Jabbah, otherwise known as 'General War' - who, you might remember, at the time fighting erupted, was head of the unit stationed outside of our HQ.

Eventually he was found and Jackson explained that the church's jeep had been taken by some of his men. Immediately, he radioed around until it was located. Within a short time Jackson was driving the vehicle out of the barracks impressed, at the captain's authority. Before he left, however, he reminded the captain of the invitation for him to attend our City Church. Perhaps we had little expectation that he would take us seriously, but much to our great surprise, on the following Sunday he appeared with his wife and children in civilian dress. He then started to attend services regularly and within a few weeks he was kneeling as a seeker and penitent at the front of the church. After the necessary lessons and counselling he was enrolled as a soldier of The Salvation Army.

Sadly, soon after being made a member, he was ambushed by some of Taylor's men who beat him up so severely that he had to be hospitalised with head wounds and brain damage. Even though Taylor, when he heard what his men had done, did pay for him to go for specialist treatment in the Ivory Coast, he never fully recovered and eventual died as a consequence of the attack.

CHAPTER 13

Advancing Out of Greater Monrovia

The problems of 1996 had not been welcome but by 1997, with Charles Taylor and the NPFL in almost total control, it was possible for elections to be held.

As expected, Charles Taylor was elected though we were told the reason for this was not necessarily because people thought he was the best candidate for the position, but rather because no one believed he would stop fighting if he lost. Having said this, hard to believe though it is, it was true that there were some who voted for him in spite of the fact that his men had killed members of their family.

For a time it now became possible to move around outside of Monrovia. Until then we had been restricted in our activities to Greater Monrovia. The only exception to that had been the time when ECOMOG troops were stationed along the road to Buchanan. However, that had just been for a matter of months in 1992. Now we were able to venture to other counties.

When it came to expanding throughout Liberia it was decided that we should start by keeping to the main roads, though 'main roads' can seem a bit of an exaggeration for major routes in Liberia. One tarred road went north through Kakata, Salala, Gbarnga and Ganta; another road went north-west to Tubmanburg; and another went south-east to Cottontree and

Buchanan. Other towns lay on dirt roads which during the rainy season were often completely unusable without a 4x4 vehicle.

My concept was that a church built at major towns along one of these three main arteries would be both visible and reachable throughout the whole year. Hopefully, these town churches would be able to fund the cost of a resident pastor. It was my belief that if churches were started in the most populated towns, with the support of Headquarters, then the members of these churches would be the ones responsible for the expansion into the villages.

At the same time as we looked to pioneering work being undertaken, it was also time for searching out our village churches that had made up the Salvation Army before the fighting tore the country apart.

The corps building in Buchanan had been properly constructed just before the war reached the town so Lieutenant William Zogar was sent to revive the Bassa-speaking church and Captain Gaymo and his wife (just promoted) was sent back to Buchanan as the divisional leaders. He was given instructions to see if an English-speaking church could be opened there, the second largest city in Liberia. It should be remembered that English was the official language in Liberia and a means of breaking down tribal barriers. We couldn't find a suitable building or land to construct a building for the English-speaking church so a large house was leased in Upper Buchanan. This became the captains' quarters, as well as the church. For a long while the captains really struggled to get more than a handful of worshippers to the English-speaking services but slowly their numbers grew, partly as a result of fighting breaking out in the interior. People seeking food and shelter fled to Buchanan.

At that time church members from places like Gbarnga gave the Upper Buchanan church greater vitality. Some of these people were musically talented and so a small choir was formed. When Sylvester, a young man from Monrovia, was sent to assist Captain Gaymo, a small elementary school was successfully started.

Leaders were also appointed to other churches in Bassa County; at Dorzohn, Kporyor, Gowingbo and Trodain. These were the villages where, before the war, there were Salvation Army churches. It was not easy for the new leaders, as these churches did not always like being under the authority of a leader appointed from Headquarters. They had been used to running things themselves and sometimes seemed only to want to be associated with The Salvation Army for material support. They eagerly accepted the new roofs for their churches as well as the milk powder and the second-hand clothing but didn't respond too well when the divisional officer asked for their tithes.

Neither did they like being corrected when syncretistic practices were observed. We even had to close one church down because they would not promise to abandon all forms of spirit worship. The leader who had been appointed to head their church had admonished them when he found that the whole village had taken part in a ceremony making oblations to spirits of the river and trees. He had urged them to renounce such conduct, but they would not. So their leader was put in charge of a small church nearby and we prayed that a true conversion would one day take place.

Before members of these churches became Salvationists, instruction had been given in the teachings contained in our Articles of Faith, together with the reasons why The Salvation

Army does not offer the Eucharist and water Baptism. But it seems their eagerness to belong to an international church for the provision of material support which they expected to follow, led them to believe that little would have to change with their ways of worship. In times of trouble there was often a temptation to try appeasing the spirits, as well as offering Christian prayers. However, it has to be said that it was often the person who had formerly been the leader of the village church who caused the biggest problems. They didn't want to surrender their authority to the movement. This led to division and splits in some of the country churches, most of which had occurred before our time in Liberia.

Nevertheless, slowly progress was made in understanding and matters of true faith. More teaching was given by the new leaders, as well as at district and national gatherings. This all helped to give a greater understanding of basic Christian doctrine and also a sense of unity of belonging to the international Salvation Army.

There were other Salvation Army churches in Gola and Kpelle-speaking districts. One of these was at Menigay, which gradually became a key village for the activities of our mobile clinic and feeding programme. When we reached this village in 1997 we had been heartened by the way its members were trying to rebuild their church which had been completely destroyed. It was a simple mud and wattle structure with a compacted mud floor. They had just completed their building up to the roof level when we reached them. They appeared to have worked harder to rebuild their church, following the effects of the war, than any of the other country churches we had visited, so we found the money to give them a corrugated zinc roof. Because zinc corroded very quickly in the salty atmosphere, aluminium would have been the material of choice but the prohibitive cost meant we we settled for aluminium-alloy as a reasonable compromise.

In Bassa, Gola and Kpelle Churches, services were conducted in the tribal language but we always found an interpreter (usually a teacher) to translate for us. The trouble was you could never be sure that you are being translated correctly, and it also made a service much longer than intended. Where translation was not needed, services usually lasted almost two hours but much longer where it was. In most of the country churches some choruses are sung in English and often, if it is a choir with students, they like to sing at least one song in English.

Though we could now drive freely all the way to Gbarnga and even all the way to Ganta, we still tried hard to be back in Monrovia before it got dark. Even in the day time there was a military base on the road, close to the town of Gbatala, where Taylor still trained his fighters and where it was rumoured dreadful torture took place. If only half of the tales about the place were true then it must have been a very evil place. Travelling back from Gbarnga on one occasion - driving fast because it was getting late - we got a puncture a couple of miles outside this notorious camp. To our surprise and disappointment, when we went to put the spare wheel on we discovered that we didn't have the special spanner to unscrew the security lock nut. We had no hammer and chisel and it took nearly an hour using rocks and metal bars to loosen the nut before the wheel could be changed and we could get back on the road again.

By then it was dark. As we approached the camp we had to stop because a check-point barrier had been set across the road. Nervously I wound down the window as a torch was shone into the cab. At first nothing was said. We were all in uniform; my wife and me plus three Liberians in our double cab. Then to my surprise, we were asked where we were going and if we could give someone a lift. In a situation like that there was no way I could say no, so I simply said, *"Jump on the back."*

He looked at the back full of building materials and muttered, *"No, go on"*.

Once out of the town a rather nervous voice from the back seat said, *"Do you know who that was who wanted a lift? He was, Jack the Rebel, the most notorious of all Taylor's killers!"*.

I think the Lord thought it was best I hadn't known!

CHAPTER 14

Command Mission Team

In December 1996 the International Youth Forum was held in South Africa and we sent Jackson Towah and Aaron Goyee to attend that event. They were two of our active young men, both of whom had been converted back at our Mamba Point quarters in early 1992.

It is hard to assess the huge effect this had on the future progress of the Command. Jackson came back spiritually inspired by the preaching of Major Chick Yuill and fired-up by Phil Wall with the concept of Mission Teams. Jackson was a natural evangelist and my wife and I always had the spiritual mission in the forefront of our activities. It was therefore not long before I was persuaded to get each of our churches in Monrovia to nominate one or two of their youth to become part of the Command Mission Team, with Jackson as their leader. Team members were not permanent, because it was hoped that after a year or so in the team members would be able to return to their own church full of evangelic zeal and be able to make a worthwhile contribution to the work in their home church. At first the team went to churches in the city to revive their open-air activities. Sadly, at church level, street evangelism was often neglected even though there were no government restrictions and it still proved to be an effective way of attracting a crowd and drawing people to church. People could even seek Christ on their knees during outdoor ministries.

The team also held campaigns reaching out especially to children, as well as doing socially caring activities like carrying water for the old people's homes. It was anticipated that a new Mission Team would be reconstituted every year though in practice it was more like every two years. The team leaders were: Jackson Towah, Momo Douwee and Ernest Ross, in that order.

The team even braved the dangers of night to go out into the worst streets of Monrovia and Paynesville to contact prostitutes and street kids. Dorothy went on several occasions to support the team in their nocturnal trips and was saddened by the sight of so many young girls selling their bodies. She was doubly sad because we had no resources, other than spiritual, at that time to do much for them. Before long the team was travelling farther afield with weekend visits to small rural churches at Bomi Hills, Mount Coffee and Menigay. By August they were seeking even greater challenges, and as the students in the team were now on holiday it was possible to stay away from Monrovia for a few days. We agreed that now there was freedom of movement in most of the country there was a need to start establishing The Salvation Army outside the confines of Monrovia, and that the town formerly used by the rebels as the centre of their activities, Gbarnga, would be an ideal place to start. It was a three hour drive, but fortunately was on a tarred road that was in reasonably good condition at that time. They decided that they would go out on Fridays and return on Sunday afternoons.

On their first trip they took letters from me to various town leaders and to the principal of the government school in the town to explain who they were and that we were an international church. This was the correct protocol. A team of unknown youths descending on a town could be wrongly interpreted, particularly as the team wore yellow tabards emblazoned with 'The Salvation Army'. To people living in a town only recently recovering from being occupied by a rebel army, the majority of whom had been young men, there was good reason for taking the precaution of letting the authorities know that they came with peaceful intent and were in fact planning to open a new church.

At their first stop in the town, a police checkpoint, they were met by a young man who immediately joined with them and took them to all the places where introductions needed to be made. This young man was a complete stranger and it was as if God had planned for him to be there because he was just what was needed in order to start the work successfully in Gbarnga. At each place Jackson explained that their intention was to open The Salvation Army Church in Gbarnga, and gave them some literature about the Army. He was received warmly by all of them and the principal of the government school agreed that they could use his school building for their services. Going regularly, holding open-airs services, visiting door-to-door and performing a pastoral care ministry, was very effective. After a few months some humble quarters were found in the centre of the town, alongside which was a concrete slab that could be used as the floor of a temporary church. Barromi and Garmai Davis, who were at that time envoys (lay pastors), were then appointed to be leaders, following a week when the Command's brass band and some other solders united to evangelise and to draw the town's attention to the Army's presence. This was the first church that was started by the Command mission team.

The team then spent some time evangelising in the next town Ganta, which is close to the Guinea border. Trouble on the road to Ganta, which was an hour from Gbarnga, stopped the team reaching it for a while and little was heard from the contact that had been made there. However, after some months word reached us from Ganta that the church there was holding services under the direction of a Salvationist who had moved there from Gbarnga. The officer from Gbarnga followed this up, and with his help the church grew. A year later I was able to enrol ten new soldiers. Not long after that an officer was appointed to pastor Ganta.

The nearest town to Monrovia of any size was Kakata but immediately after the cessation of fighting it was more like a ghost town. Nearly all the buildings were in ruins and some had trees growing inside them. Many of the houses had been built out of mud blocks and only thinly plastered. Once damaged, it doesn't take long before such buildings disintegrate during the heavy rains. The town had suffered badly at the beginning of the war and most of the inhabitants had fled. It then became occupied by rebel forces. When, in 1995, rebels were allowed into the capital, very few of the original inhabitants hurried back. But after the opening of Gbarnga Church it was decided that it would be good if the Army could establish a presence in Kakata, and so the Mission Team began to hold various outdoor activities in the town.

However, it was not easy to find somewhere to hold Sunday services. In the end we had to lease a house belonging to a Lebanese trader (a relative of Tony Hage). It was not ideal because there was no large room for a service, but it was the best we could find. Once we found a house it created a complication because we then had to find someone to put in charge of it. What we decided to do was to send out three young men who had just graduated from the L.M. school: Cyrus Sneh (who went on to train as one of our first P.A.'s); Elijah Sowen (who taught

Religious studies and was also given a sponsorship for teacher training) and Samuel Jubor, (who became the registrar at the W.B. School). For almost three months they lived in the leased building and worked hard to continue the work started by the Mission Team They conducted outdoor evangelism and gave training to the new recruits. By the time Lieutenants Anthony and Munah Sio returned from their commissioning in Ghana and took charge of the church at Kakata there was a vibrant group of new Salvationists with junior and senior choirs.

Meanwhile we had received a letter from Zwedru, former President Samuel Doe's county town, three hundred miles from Monrovia. The letter contained a request for us to send an officer, Bibles, uniforms and song books, as there was now a Salvation Army church holding services in that town. The letter was signed by Shad Joloe, a young man who had fled from Monrovia in 1996 when fighting broke out in the city. He was a former student of our Len Millar School in Monrovia and had been living in the barracks, but that became a very dangerous place to be for members of his tribe, the Krahn. He had been a Salvationist at the City Church and had been awarded the Bible prize when he graduated from the L.M. School. Like a lot of other Krahn, he had opted to return to his home county. On another sheet of paper he had listed the Salvationists in his congregation at Zwedru. Ten of them had been enrolled in the City Church, having fled the capital as he had, and two had been enrolled while refugees in the Budumburum camp in Ghana. The church in the camp was opened by William Sackie, a Liberian, while he was on out-training in Ghana.

Easter holidays were coming up in a couple of months, so we planned to get to Zwedru by then and take the Mission Team with us. We set out using our Land Rover jeep and the large Toyota pickup which had just been delivered via a container from England. We had no idea what we were heading into, and how we got the pickup as far as Tapita, half-way from Ganta to Zwedru, I shall never know.

The journey from Monrovia to Ganta was quite good, with tarred road all the way. From there onward it was what is normally called a dirt road. Before the war, we were told it was regularly graded but it had had no maintenance for at least seven years. The rainy season had been well under way for over a month. Time and again the mission team had to get out and push the pickup through the deep muddy water, sometimes taking almost an hour to get through stretches of the road. When we started out, not being very experienced driving in such conditions, I frequently got stuck. But then, following the advice of an aid worker who we met on the way, I started to choose the line I was going to take and then put my foot down and kept it down. At times it was scary, as the jeep sometimes leaned precariously to one side and on others occasions almost went along sideways. When water got into the pickup's air filter, smoke (or steam, I was never quite sure which) billowed from the exhaust pipe. However, with me driving madly and the pickup being dug/pushed out, we eventually reached the town of Tapita, where we decided to spend the night. Knowing we had been taking liberties with the pickup we decided to leave it in Tapita with the majority of the Mission Team, who were utterly exhausted. They were left to evangelise in Tapita and then to return in convoy with us on our way back from Zwedru.

The Salvationists in Zwedru had heard that we were coming because we had sent a message by the Red Cross radio, but we were a day late and there was no one to meet us. But it was not long before the word reached the members and we were quickly surrounded by the Zwedru Salvationists. On the Sunday we were surprised to find a worshipping congregation, started by our school graduate, of more than forty adults. Jackson had left the team in Tapita and came along with us, as his home village was on our route. We had all stopped briefly with him to greet his relatives. In Zwedru, he spoke the local dialect, so quickly organised the members to hold a march of witness and an open-air service before the Sunday meeting. Less than a year later we sent Lieutenants Amos and Janet Diah to take charge of the church; being from the same tribe as the people in Zwedru was a valuable asset to their ministry. This was thought to be the wisest policy, following the problems between this tribe and Charles Taylor's militia. Later, in 2001when the family had to flee from the town, this proved to have been a judicious decision.

Returning through Tapita we found the Mission Team had paraded the streets dressed in the clothes they had taken for their Easter drama. This had attracted a lot of attention and curiosity which, following their performances, convicted many who stepped forward to claim Christ. It would seem that splitting up our troops had all been part of God's plan to reach more people with the Gospel. We got back safely and were greatly relieved to discover there was no damage to our new pickup other than a mud and water-filled air-filter.

How people found their way in the forests of the interior I never quite understood but matters were made worse for everyone when the logging companies (mostly from the Far East) started to decimate the forests. Wide new dirt roads were driven deep into the forests, creating new highways in the middle of nowhere. Those that coincided with our route were fine but often they obliterated the established roads. On one occasion returning from Zwedru, we travelled for 45 minutes before a boy we passed told us that we were simply heading toward a lumber camp.

In 2000 Jackson went with us to the Millennium Congress in Atlanta. We had expected him to have gone on to the Eastern Territory's School for Officer Training but instead he returned to get married and then went back to the States to get a degree in Divinity and Counselling, moving on to achieve a Masters in Company Law. He is now a Salvationist in the USA. We were sorry to loose him and very disappointed that he never became a Salvation Army officer because he was a fine leader and evangelist.

Momo Duwee, who was from Bushrod Island Church and still studying at the W.B. High School, took over the leadership of the Mission Team from Jackson. He too received some training experience outside Liberia as we sent him to join a team in South Africa for evangelism at the All Africa Games. He then stayed on a bit longer for added training.

He took our Mission Team to Tubmanburg; an hour-and-a-half drive to the north-west of Monrovia. This was a bold move for it was known that the anti-Taylor militia, called LURD, were not far from the town. As soon as the team arrived they met a former Salvationist from the Bushrod Island Church and within a few weeks they were having more than twenty adults to their Sunday meetings with the same number of children. A building was quickly rented, repaired and occupied, with new recruits working together to get everything in a fit state for worship. As usual they were very conscientious in visiting the sick and grieving.

It was while they were visiting one of their contacts in the local clinic that they over heard a rather shocking conversation. A

LURD fighter who was seriously wounded, was being visited by another rebel on crutches. To Momo's horror, he heard the rebel in the bed boasting about how he and others had eaten the heart of one of Taylor's soldiers. The youth on crutches, though from the same rebel faction, showed disgust at this and told his friend that he could never do such a thing. Sensing that there was some hope of winning the lad on crutches for the Lord, Momo overtook him as he left the clinic and invited him to come to the quarters for a talk. He did come, and following this began to attend services regularly. Within a short time was soundly converted, and freely confessed his sin before everyone; he repented from ever going to fight again.

This presented a problem. He explained that as soon as his leg, through which a bullet had passed, healed, the militia would expect him back. If he did not return he would be called a traitor who could be hunted down and killed at any time. While his leg was improving he was active with the Tubmanburg Church but it eventually became clear that he would have to find a place of safety. We decided that the W.B. School would be the best place for him, as it was surrounded by an eight foot wall. It would also have the added advantage that Prince Padmore (that was his name) would then be able to complete his spiritual and academic education. At the time of writing he leads his Paynesville Corps Mission Team and, with the support of a Salvationist couple in England, is studying at the Methodist University. When he graduates, and finds a wife, he hopes to become a Salvation Army officer.

Once it was clear that a corps had been firmly established at Tubmanburg I looked for someone to lead it on a more permanent basis. I had no spare officers. Finally Momo Douwee agreed to stay on in the town with another team member, Dennis Krah, as envoys. Sadly the Tubmanburg Church suffered a big set back when the LURD forces attacked and captured the town. Interestingly, as people fled the town, most of the Salvationists stayed together in uniform as they moved out. They rested for a while at a small town called Klay, where Momo managed to get away and into Monrovia with an appeal to us for help to be sent to Klay for the Tubmanburg Salvationists. They needed to get assistance for them to pass the checkpoint, which had been set up to prevent Monrovia getting flooded with displaced people.

Ernest Ross drove the jeep back to Klay with some blankets and food but though he managed to talk his way past the checkpoint he was only able to collect Dennis and two or three other Salvationists before crowds started to jump in and onto the vehicle. He therefore got out as quickly as he could.

The following week the rebels attacked again and the population of Tubmanburg broke through the checkpoint and fled again toward Monrovia. The UN set up a camp for them, north-west of the city, and close to the St. Paul River. This place was called V.O.A. because the USA had had a relay station for their international radio broadcasts there before the war.

With Momo and Dennis safe in Monrovia I appointed them to share the leadership at Gardnersville where there had been a leadership breakdown. After three weeks, however, Dennis came to ask if he could be appointed to the camp at V.O.A. to look after the members of the Tubmanburg Church who were now in that camp for I.D.P.'s. This was a great act of love for his people, as it meant he would live in terrible conditions in a hut that he would have to build for himself. After praying with him and making sure he had considered all the implications of such a move, he went with our blessing and stayed there, for more than two years helping his people build a temporary church. Eventually the camp was disbanded and people were able to return to Tubmanburg. Momo continued to run the Gardnersville Church and when he was made a lieutenant the ladies in his church honoured him by laying down their lappers for him to walk on. The CSM admitted that when Momo had been appointed he had great reservations as to the likely competency of this 'boy' to lead this rather volatile church, but he had proved himself to be a strong and godly young man who had earned the respect of the whole church.

Both these young men had shown what had become the expectation for members of the Command Mission Team: a love for the people, evangelical zeal and true spirituality. As one community leader expressed to me; "*When these young men descended on the town we thought they would bring trouble. Such groups in the past have come with guns, and had been drunkards and womanizers, but your young men had brought a true caring Christian church to us - we love them.*"

To choose a new leader for the Mission Team when Momo and Dennis were left behind in Tubmanburg was not an easy decision. For a brief time Ernest Suah led them but this did not prove ideal so, after taking advice from a few trusted Liberian officers, it was decided that Ernest Ross was the best candidate for the role. As I have already explained, he had been with the Salvation Army almost from the first day of our arrival and about two years later had arrived in our yard carrying all his possessions in a small carrier bag. In his hand was a note from his father. The note was brief, saying that he was leaving town to go back to his job in the forest and sending Ernest to me as the boy wanted to be a pastor in our church one day and all he was interested in was The Salvation Army. We knew that the woman Ernest's father had been living with was not his true mother, though she had been treating him reasonably well. So this sad little figure was welcomed onto the compound and stayed with his 'brother' Jackson. He grew up quickly as a strong, mature and loyal Salvationist, as well as an intelligent student at school and college. It was to him who we now turned to lead our Command Mission Team.

For a time it was not safe to go very far out of Monrovia but after a while it was decided that they would attempt to start a church at Salala, a town just under two hours drive from the city. Once again all the courtesies were observed, visiting all the town dignitaries including the 'joint forces unit' that was in military control of the town. They even found the owner of a school willing to let them use her building for Sunday worship. It was not long before The Salvation Army made real progress in the town, so much so that some of the local churches went to the town superintendent and asked him to have it banished from Salala. He responded by saying that he would rather throw all of them out and keep the young Salvationists. The Bible, he said, instructed people to feed the hungry, visit those in prison, care for the sick and comfort those who mourn, and he had seen the Salvation Army doing just that when the local churches were doing nothing.

Happily, it wasn't long before the majority of Salala's local churches were working well together and within a year of an officer being appointed to Salala he was elected as the town's President of the United Churches' Fellowship.

It should be noted that these young men who formed the Command Mission Team were well-balanced young people who had learned how to enjoy life without going to the excesses that so many of their peers in Liberia were sliding into. It was not uncommon for them to play members of the local community at soccer which, as most people know, is the national sport all over Africa, not just Liberia. But the team used such times of recreation to build bridges between themselves and the local people. It was not surprising therefore, that sometimes they had soccer matches against members of the combined forces who were garrisoned in Salala.

On one occasion Ernest played for the combined forces against the Mission Team and was congratulated for playing fairly and saving them from an ignominious defeat (some of them were not completely sober). Some of the militia later began to attend services and on at least two occasions this trust and respect that was built up was of great benefit to The Salvation Army and Ernest personally.

It was not all fun and games for them, however, as there were still many dangers for anyone who travelled out of Monrovia. On one trip to Salala they were waiting to be waved through at a checkpoint when tempers flared up between the two separate rebel factions guarding the post. Guns were raised and cocked, so, with the cry to those in the back of the pick-up of "*Keep your heads down; I'm making a dash for it.*" Ernest put his foot on the accelerator and drove the vehicle forward without waiting for any permission. They didn't hesitate to return the following week as planned.

When, in 2003 LURD rebels got into Monrovia via the St. Paul Bridge, Ernest tried to get through a Government checkpoint at night to rescue Captain Jallayu, our corps officer there. Eventually he was forced to turn back as the soldiers would not let him pass at the checkpoint. What made it worse was that one of the soldiers took his mobile phone from him. Ernest, annoyed and upset, went looking for the officer-in-charge of the checkpoint guards. Finally he found him and, to his great surprise, he turned out to be the officer who had been Joint Forces Commander at Salala. He told Ernest not to worry because by the morning he would get it back for him - and he did! The next day Ernest was both successful in collecting the corps officer and getting his cell phone back.

On another occasion about six months later when things had mostly calmed down, Ernest was driving back from the newest corps that his team was starting at Cotton Tree when he saw people angrily stoning every vehicle that passed along the road. Not wanting to have our jeep damaged, he drew into the curb some distance away and walked up to where the riot was going on. When he went to ask the reason for the trouble, he found he was talking to another soldier with whom he had played soccer. The soldier recognised Ernest straight away and greeted him as a friend. Ernest explained that he wanted to pass by on the road and the soldier said he should just drive through and no harm would come to him or his jeep. As soon as Ernest reached the stone-throwing scene, the order was given to let The Salvation Army jeep through and they simply waved it by. These were just another couple of the times when the Lord showed He had gone ahead of His people.

After the Mission Team had been running Salala Corps for just over a year, newly commissioned officers, Captains Willamena and Jonathan Walker, were appointed to the church. Within just two weeks the captain came to Command Headquarters to say what a fine job the 'boys' had done in that town. He was amazed to find that he had been given an active church, with almost thirty enrolled soldiers and seven acting local officers. He also marvelled at the way the members knew almost as many Army songs (hymns) as he did, and that so many of his soldiers were in uniform. Such praise was deserved, but rarely given. This captain had been a pioneer at Greenville himself as an envoy, and knew what such results represented by way of devotion to the divine cause.

After a short pause a new Mission Team was formed with Ernest still as its leader, with some old and some new members. The town chosen for them to begin a work in was 'Cotton Tree'- named I presume, after the huge trunk of a cotton tree which, until 2003, stood at the entrance to the town. It has now been cut down to the ground as it was becoming a danger to local people and buildings. This town is on the edge of the Firestone Rubber Plantation and about ninety minutes drive from Monrovia. It is also almost midway between Buchanan and Monrovia. Up to this time there had never been any Salvation Army church along this route. It was therefore a strategic centre for the Army to be represented.

When we had first passed through this district in 1992 on our way to Buchanan, there had only been twenty to thirty houses and stores but now there were hundreds of small, properly constructed, cement block houses. I can only guess that one of the reasons for this was that since late 1996, due to its proximity to the International airport, first ECOMOG and then UNIMIL had always kept a strong military presence in the area. This meant it was one of the safe areas of Liberia. The fact that many of the people building in this area were, or had been, employed by Firestone Rubber Co. was certainly another reason why development was taking place in this district. This recent upsurge in building did make finding a location for the Mission Team in which to begin their activities, including services, very difficult. Eventually, after a few weeks when only open-air and door-to-door evangelism was possible, a man did offer the team a small space in the middle of a densely populated part of the town.

Once again it was not long before the new converts were able to work with the team to build a tarpaulin and bamboo structure in which to hold their services. It was never easy as the space was small and there were a large number of children to cope with as well as thirty to forty adults. Eventually the children had to be given their own programme in the kitchen of the house next to the church. After about a year the team was able to pass the church on to a cadet couple for their out-training.

It was expected that the Mission Team would continue to go forward to fresh fields but when the new Command leaders arrived it ceased operation because, I was told, it lacked the provision of the necessary logistics.

In 2002 I had asked all of our corps to try to start a mission team at church level. Several of them succeeded in this, and the 2004 Youth Councils included a competition between corps mission teams. This included giving a record of their last four months' activities, acting out a mini open-air service, a marching display, and a quiz based on two books: the book of Genesis and another about William Booth. By the time of the councils, Paynesville team was active at Mount Barclay, St. Paul Bridge at New Kru Town, Gardnersville at Barnesville, Zwedru at Zleh Town and Salala at Flelah. Each of these centres, started by corps mission teams, is now operating as an active church.

Whilst writing about mission teams I should like to include the opening up of Greenville corps, which was done by a one-man team because it was far too distant from Monrovia (almost 200 miles) to have been worked by the Mission Team at weekends. Greenville is a port south-east of Buchanan, used mostly for the export of timber. It was in a county where we had no church, and so we desired to open the work there and I felt that it would help if we had someone who could speak the county dialect. I then discovered that one of our envoys who had recently had to flee from Gbarnga had, as a boy, lived in that tribal area and could speak their dialect. Envoy Jonathan Walker had a strong faith and had always been prepared to go wherever his services were required, so I invited him to accept the challenge of starting the work in Greenville. Initially, it meant leaving his wife and young child behind in Monrovia; they were to follow once accommodation suitable for a family had been found.

We took him and a very few basic items to Greenville and one hour later we drove off, leaving him to start The Salvation Army in that town. In that hour we had managed to find someone to rent him a room. Apart from that we could give him little assistance and the nearest church and officer support was 100 miles away in Zwedru. God honoured this step of faith and just opposite the house in which we had found him a room a carpenter offered space for a temporary church. Within a couple of weeks a congregation was worshiping, and within six weeks new recruits were busy constructing a bamboo church.

On the occasions I was able to visit I used to take a group of young men (mostly hostel boys) who called themselves 'Colonel Brian's Mission Team'. They would fill up the hours with person-to-person evangelism, particularly around the town's one and only video club. One of these trips was particularly memorable. The boys slept in the one room rented for the envoy but we had to sleep in the only place we could find. It was a room in a large ruin of a house that had no facilities at all. We made our way to the room by torchlight. There was a thin double mattress on the floor, which we thought would at least be better than sleeping in the jeep. That was a mistake because we got little sleep that night. To start with the windows were closed to keep the mosquitoes out which made it stifling hot. In spite of that the room was still full of mosquitoes. This meant that the cotton sleeping bags that we always took with us had to be tucked in around our heads, making us even hotter. But there was worse! As soon as the noise quietened down outside we began to hear other sounds. Because the floor boards were old and splintered, the owner had covered the boards with a tarpaulin sheet but under that sheet it seems there lived a family of rats. All through the night we could hear them running around under the tarpaulin; right up to our mattress. In Liberia rats were known to chew people's toes (I had been shown examples). So, as soon as dawn came we were up and out of the building, adamant that we would never return to it again

Eventually a large house was rented for the envoy's quarters and after being re-roofed and having considerable time and money spent on it, a good home was provided for the him and his wife. Since that time Greenville town has on different occasions been cut off from Headquarters by rebel activities, but under Lieutenant Isaac Bodioh they quickly recovered and reached out into the surrounding districts.

CHAPTER 15

The City Hall Land Saga

The saga of the land opposite the Municipal City Hall was a fight that lasted for six years. It wasn't a physical battle in the sense of guns and rockets nor was a spiritual one in terms of trouble in the church; this was a legal and political battle. It began as a simple property dispute but escalated into a six-year legal case, being taken to the highest court in the land, as well as my arrest and interviews with the Minister of Justice.

It all started in November 1995, when Mr. Payne, a respected businessman, came to my office with an offer to sell a building situated on more than an acre of land opposite the Municipal City Hall. At that time we had wanted to expand the Len Millar School and it seemed an ideal spot for such a purpose. Moreover, being so close to the centre of town and to the Liberia University, I thought it would be an ideal site for our own university one day. The potential was obvious, more for the land than for the property. The amount being asked for was not large but the Command did not have anywhere near such a sum available.

However, being convinced of the future value to the Army of such a site and the bargain price being asked, I applied though our Territorial Commander in Ghana to our International Headquarters, for a special grant. To my great surprise and pleasure they also saw the purchase as an investment for our future work and did not take long before agreeing to the special grant. Our surveyors had already checked out the genuine nature of the deal so as soon as word reached us of IHQ's positive decision we set the wheels in motion, through our counsellor, for the purchase of the property.

Careful checking of the authenticity of deeds was very important because buying land is fraught with many dangers in Liberia. Sometimes the same piece of land will be sold several times to the incautious, or someone will sell someone else's land, using fraudulent deeds. But I had been in direct communication with the owner, Mrs. Victoria Johnson, a woman in her eighties, living in the USA. She was able to assure me that she had the current deeds, which we confirmed by carrying out a search at the National Archives. We saw one problem, and that was the present occupier, but, as Mr. Payne had the vendor's power of attorney, we accepted his assurance that a legal eviction would be a simple task. To be on the safe side I withheld some of the purchase price until we had obtained vacant possession. As it turned out, it was a wise decision.

We soon discovered that the occupier was the original legal counsellor (solicitor) for the owner and, at the time of the proposed purchase, was also the acting Attorney General for the transitional government. He claimed that he had bought the property from the venerable lady in America. Actually he had simply told her that the building was damaged beyond repair, which was untrue, and that he would send her some African goods (mostly African traditional clothing valued at US$3,000) in exchange for the land and property. Though this message had been sent to her there had never been any agreement, and the land was still hers to use or sell as she pleased. However, this point now had to be settled in court. We had the deeds of ownership, but he was in residence.

While the deeds were being probated and letters were going back and forth to the counsellor and the lady in the USA, we did not try to enter the building. Unfortunately, while we were in the process of applying for a court order to evict the counsellor, war entered the city and normal government ceased for a time. This was the occasion when Dorothy and I were evacuated out of the country by helicopter.

When we returned in August 1996, we were granted a court order and Mr. Payne hired policemen to evict the residents along with their possessions. I then sent Jackson along with our carpenter to nail up all the doors, except one. Two young men were then delegated to use the unlocked room and to be security for the building. Within a couple of hours another group of policemen, hired by the counsellor, arrived to reinstate those evicted. They then proceeded to obtain arrest warrants which accused several Salvationists, who he knew by name, of stealing thousands of dollars of goods from the people residing in the building when the police had evicted them. We only learned about this when we heard loud banging on the gates of our HQ and a voice demanding my presence, yelling out that they had a summons for my arrest. I later discovered that this is a common trick played on innocent people to extort money following an eviction. It was a real puzzle why they had arrived calling out my name, as I had not even entered the building and it had been genuine policemen who had done the evicting.

Our property manager, Mr. Bainda, whose name was also on the summons, went to speak with them, telling them how ridiculous the accusations were, but they wouldn't leave. So I decided to make as if to go with them, but in my mind I intended to drive to The Salvation Army's legal counsellor. At first I had a big struggle with them as they tried to force me to give them my car keys, but I managed to get seated in my pick-up and said I would drive myself to the court. Eventually it was agreed that Mr. Bainda and I would go, taking some police with us in my vehicle with the rest of the police following behind in their pick-up. When we got close to the turning for the road to the court, I increased speed and made a dash for the lawyer's office. I got out and began to climb the stairs to his office but a policeman grabbed me and hauled me back into their truck while I shouted, trying to attract the attention of our counsellor. In our pickup cab the police major wrestled with me, trying to force me to hand over the keys to my vehicle but I believed if they got their hands on it I would probably never see it again. I managed to retain my grip on the keys but in doing so sustained bruises from the police major wielding his walkie-talkie on my hands and legs. I later found out that the 'major' was the nephew of the counsellor we were trying to evict. When someone called out that the counsellor was not in his office, I reluctantly agreed to leave my vehicle where it was, still clutching my keys, and got into their pick-up to be driven to the Palace of Justice.

While I was being hauled off to court, two other things were set in motion. Dorothy, my wife, was a little stunned at first but didn't panic. She contacted Tony Hage (always a lifeline for us) and explained things to him. He told her not to worry, he would sort it out and would be at the Palace of Justice within minutes and he added, "*This shouldn't be happening, leave it to me.*" Just as she put the phone down Jackson arrived home from school with a number of Salvationist youths. When he heard what had happened he hurried off with the lads saying "*Don't worry, we'll get him back*".

Seeing the emotions were high she was quick to call out as they left in the jeep, "*Don't forget we're The Salvation Army*"!

True to his word, Tony was quick in getting to the court and I could hear him admonishing some of the arresting policemen's party who were standing in the corridor. He immediately got in contact with his personal lawyer, who appeared within minutes because he was already on the premises. Within a short while it became clear that we would be granted bail fairly quickly on the deposit of a substantial bond, but the paperwork took time.

Meanwhile, Jackson in the meanwhile, with his group of angry young men, headed straight for the Ministry of Justice building, mistakenly thinking that was where we would be taken. When they arrived, they all poured out of the jeep shouting that their 'father' should be released. The guards, seeing a stream of youths heading for the door and shouting as they came, simply disappeared. They mistook them for a rebel faction and didn't wait to see if they were armed (which of course they were not). Rushing into every room in the building and finding I was not there they took off again, this time to the Palace of Justice where we were being held. Fortunately we knew they were coming, as police officers had radioed through to the court officials telling them what had happened and what to expect. I say '*fortunately*' because it gave me time to ask Tony to go down to meet them and explain that we would soon be released and that I was okay. I did not want them to come charging in to attempt a rescue!

Jackson, to satisfy himself that we were safe, did come up but did not bring anyone with him and for that I was grateful. By the evening we were all back home, a little dazed and bemused at the events of the day. I had known that people could easily get imprisoned for no good reason, as on several occasions I had been to the Central Police Station to beg or pay for the release of a person I believed to be innocent. However, I never believed it would happen to me - but it had!

I learned later that the counsellor's nephew did not get off without punishment, for when Jackson took some people home in the evening they passed him. Though it was dark, they recognised him straightaway. The jeep was stopped, and once again with cries condemning the actions against their 'father' they grabbed him and roughed him up a little. I do not condone such actions, of course, but I understood the emotions that drove them to do it. Fortunately he was not badly hurt and the next day his main complaint to the ECOMOG checkpoint guards, who watched the incident, was that his radio had been thrown away.

Meanwhile, I lodged a formal complaint to the Minister of Justice for the treatment I had received from the police, as I now had the evidence on my hands and legs. Places where I had received blows from the police major's handset had, overnight, developed into large black and blue bruises. When I came before the minister she called for the counsellor, who was in an office just down the corridor, and she asked him who had been in charge of the officers sent to serve the summons. He explained that it was his nephew, a major in the police force. Questioned further about the major, he had to admit that he was not really a major nor did he have the authority to undertake such work. When he tried to justify the treatment I had received by pointing out that his nephew had been beaten-up the following evening by friends of mine, her surprising reply was; '*Sometimes you just have to meet force with force*'.

The counsellor was then given a stern warning and the minister gave me an apology on behalf of the government. Nothing ever became of the charges levied against us, and we did eventually get the deeds of our headquarters back which, on the day of the arrest, we had to leave as a bond.

It gave me a good feeling when the counsellor was cautioned, but we still did not have access to our property. A General in NPFL came to me, having heard of our difficulty, and offered to get them out for me but I just thanked him and explained that I preferred to stick to the courts rather than resort to violence. It has to be remembered that there was little firm rule of law at this time in the capital, and many issues were still being settled by intimidation and force of arms.

For us, however, the next step was to hire a specialist lawyer. Sadly, having accepted some of our money he decided he wanted to be a politician, and went off to Ghana to the conferences being held there to decide the nature of Liberia's future government. This lost us a full year, as well as a few hundred US dollars. In the end we started again with another lawyer, who informed us that the counsellor had managed somehow to register a 'caveat' on the original probation of our deeds. Fortunately the judge who had probated the deeds was now one of the judges who had to pass judgment on its veracity. I'm not sure if she reclused herself, but she would certainly have been able to confirm that the caveat must have been submitted well after the deeds had been through the court.

With that concern out of the way, we then went to court before a judge and a fifteen-person jury to establish our legal ownership of the property. Though the counsellor was no longer the Attorney General, he knew all the tricks of his trade, and used them time and again to drag out proceedings. He used a variety of excuses, including having to arrive late in court because he was also involved, on behalf of the government, in prosecuting rebel soldiers. Eventually, the jury did get sent out to consider their verdict and, miraculously returned in just two days with a unanimous decision in favour of The Salvation Army. I say '*miraculously*' because unanimous verdicts are hard to obtain in Liberia.

It was with no great surprise we heard a few days later that the court's decision had been appealed against, and would now have to go before the Supreme Court. Here again we were at a grave disadvantage because one member of the bench was a cousin of the counsellor, and he did not recluse himself. It was also very expensive to engage a counsellor to fight the case for us at Supreme Court level, but all things considered we were not over-charged, bearing in mind the fact that the case was heard three times in three years, but each time no decision was handed down. Everyone present at the hearings agreed that The Salvation Army's case was cast-iron, but was probably being blocked by the relative of the counsellor. Naturally we were spending a lot of money without being given any judgment, so to say we were getting very frustrated would be an understatement.

The case had now taken six years, but in one way it had not been a disaster because we had no immediate need for the land. However, we had now applied to Norway (The Salvation Army and Norwegian Government - NORAD) for money to build a teacher training college and the only land we really had for it was this land opposite the City Hall; which as I have already mentioned, is conveniently close to the Liberia University. I therefore decided to try another way to get a decision from the court; with the help of one of our school instructors who had many contacts because of his work for press and radio, I had a meeting with the Minister for Presidential Affairs. Knowing that our cause was just, I had no conscience on appealing to him to get the President Taylor to see that we were treated justly and fairly. I was most surprised that he did not ask for anything for himself only that The Salvation Army should try to start working in his home county.

Within a month we had our ruling and took possession of the property. Within two months of us taking ownership of the land, NORAD had awarded us the grant to build a teacher training college. It had taken six years to obtain the land, but the timing was just right.

I have to admit there had been times during those years when I had wondered if we would end up victorious in our battle to win the rights of ownership, for many people inside and out of The Salvation Army had prophesied a negative outcome. But in the end our commitment to the cause was rewarded, and God's timing was perfect - as it always is of course! When all the litigation costs and payments were added together, we had still paid less than one hundred thousand US dollars for a large building and more than an acre of land in a prime position. Even considering all the heartache, intimidation and harassment we had gone through, we still knew we had made an excellent bargain for which future generations would marvel and praise God.

One last hurdle that needed overcoming cropped up when the UN (who had 15,000 soldiers in Liberia) decided that they needed the land for their operations. They pointed out that if they went to the government they felt sure they would be granted the land for the duration of their stay, which was likely to be many years.

But by negotiation we were able to plan the position for our building in such a way that room was left for their needs as well as ours. It was also agreed that they would refurbish and use the old building on the land, and after the first year pay us a rent while they were occupying it. At the time of writing it gives me considerable pleasure to know that the college is now fully operational and has been opened as a vocational training college.

CHAPTER 16

Here Come the Generals

On January 1, 1997 Liberia became a 'Command' - making it independent of Ghana and directly answerable to The Salvation Army's leaders in its London-based International Headquarters.

It was also a momentous year for the State of Liberia, as elections were to be held which it was hoped would bring lasting peace. But tensions were high. Elections in Africa, particularly after such a bloody civil war, can lead to a lot of in-fighting and bloodshed. Being a nation steeped in superstitions of every kind, it was also a time when people, even children, could go missing, to be found later with body parts missing. Supernatural powers were being sought to gain electoral victory. The main participants in this electoral battle were Charles Taylor and Helen Johnson-Sirleaf. Charles Taylor won very easily with 75% of the votes and no need for any runoff.

Soon after hearing that we were to be given command status, we also learned that a proposal had been put forward for the head of the international Salvation Army, General Paul Rader, with his wife Commissioner Frances Rader, to visit Liberia in that same year. Such an honour could not be refused, but the state of the country was a worry.

Our biggest fear was the possibility that Taylor might not win the election and that he would return to fighting. This would be a disaster, as he had many of his men already in Monrovia. However, we need not had been anxious on that score because the people also feared such a consequence and therefore gave him a comfortable election victory, and so prevented him and his men going on the rampage.

One sign that Taylor was taking every precaution to assure his election was discovered following a telephone call I made to Tony Hage about the arrangements we were making for General Rader's arrival. Shortly after putting the phone down, Tony had a visit from a senior official from Taylor's residence. He came 'requesting' Tony to come with him immediately. Though Tony and Charles Taylor knew each other quite well it was still an unusual summons.

Tony therefore went straight off to Taylor's mansion, not completely at ease, for people had been known to have gone in and not seen to come out. However, all ended satisfactorily when Tony was able to tell President Taylor what his conversation talking about 'the visit of the General' was referring to. It seems that the phone lines of either The Salvation Army or Tony, or both, were being tapped. The mention of the term 'general' and 'the visit of the general' had caused some concern in Taylor's camp, as an attempted coup was always a possibility in Liberia. When the truth was known Tony was able to return home unharmed. This taught us, however, to be very careful what we said over the phone. It was possible that any uncomplimentary remarks relating to Taylor or his regime could have landed us up in prison and, bearing in mind what happened when I clashed with the factional Minister of Education, possibly the closure of The Salvation Army's activities in Liberia.

General Paul Rader

By the time General Rader actually arrived Taylor was officially President and the atmosphere had calmed down. Many Salvationists travelled to welcome him at the city airport (the international airport was still closed) and Ghanaian military aircraft flew overhead in what appeared to be a salute to him though this was never confirmed.

It was a very joyous occasion, when normal formalities were brief. Everyone wanted to touch the General and his wife which at first I think they found a little disconcerting but soon went with the flow. When Oral, one of our hostel boys, grabbed the document bag from the aid-de-camp, Major Marvell, I think he almost had a fit but I was quickly able to assure him of its safety and that it was a traditional courtesy.

We had hoped that Taylor would have given the general an audience, but at the very last minute were informed very politely that the president would not be able to see the general as he was going to be in Buchanan. Our interview with the media could not be called a success either, because it seemed that mostly it was only youths who turned up. However, at least one of them represented a news broadcaster and another was from a daily newspaper. The others were mostly from school news teams.

The meetings with the officers and leaders went well, and the numbers at soldiers' gatherings were so numerous they even surprised me. On the site of the William Booth School, which was still under construction, the general was able to unveil a commemorative plaque. We hadn't long opened the girls' hostel and so a visit there was included, to the delight of the girls who all wanted a picture taken with Mrs. Rader. She kindly obliged them and climbed on one of their bunk beds for me to take the photographs. The general and his wife entered into the informal atmosphere of the occasion in a very relaxed and cheerful manner. After seeing the girls we went on to the boys' hostel, and a few of them were able to challenge the general to a game of table tennis. I think he surprised them by his skill at the game.

The one problem of the visit didn't occur in Liberia. The general had quite a tight timetable to keep as he was going straight to Ghana on leaving Liberia. He was scheduled to conduct the commissioning ceremony on the following day, and was to be the speaker at the pre-commissioning meeting the evening before, the same day that he was leaving Liberia! When the Air Ivoire plane touched down at Abidjan Airport, everyone was asked to get out. Mrs. Rader had been sleeping and when she was woken she asked if they had reached Ghana yet. On being told they hadn't, she said that she was staying on board, not knowing that everyone had been told to alight from the plane. The steward was rather harsh in telling her that she must get out to change planes.

This was an unscheduled change of aircraft, and we all began to suspect the worst. The aircraft had been requisitioned by the president or a senior politician; when it would be back was anyone's guess. The general now feared that he would not be in time for that evening's meeting, and was concerned for those who would be waiting for him. He asked his aide-de-camp to see if he could be put on another flight but he was left with no alternative but to sit and wait the return of the original aircraft. We arrived in Accra too late for that evening meeting, but was greeted by the Territorial Commander for Ghana, Colonel Amoah, and several very relieved Salvationists who had feared that there might have been trouble in Liberia.

As the dignitaries were whisked away into the VIP lounge Dorothy and I had to make our own way to the arrivals section, ready to face a bit of a grilling because we didn't have a valid entry visa. We had travelled with the General to Ghana because two Liberians, who we had sent for training, were included with the cadets who were to be commissioned. With the help of Kofi, the Army's protocol secretary, we were allowed in after the payment of a substantial fee.

General John Gowans

General Rader had arrived in Monrovia when we were enjoying a brief time of peace after Charles Taylor had been voted into power.

In January of 2002 things had already taken a turn for the worse. A new faction called LURD had come on to the scene, made up of many of the old ULIMO 'J' faction. They had advanced very close to the outskirts of Monrovia at St. Paul Bridge. However, as the advance seemed stalled, the decision was made on a balance of risks, that General Gowans would be safe for the brief time of his visit. He was only coming for three days and I believed that if the rebels did manage to cross the St. Paul River we would still have time to get the general out. But to say things were tense would be an understatement!

At the airport we were not the only group who had come to await the arrival of their church leader. However, just as our leader was arriving the other group was being told that their leader had decided not to come because of the dangerous situation in the country. One of them congratulated us on our leader's bravery in coming at such a precarious time. I didn't tell them that our leader, whilst knowing there were dangers in Liberia, did not know what the latest threats were on Monrovia and how close the rebels were to entering the city.

The Robertsfield International Airport was now being used, but the chaos that met every arriving passenger was little better than had been experienced at Spriggs Payne Airport in the city. After a very patient general had got through the custom formalities, during which he had to bend down to fill in his entry forms on his knee, he was met outside by the brass band and a happy singing group of Salvationists with flags waving. He was then driven to Monrovia by Tony Hage, who supplied the transport.

Weeks before the general's arrival we had booked rooms for him, Commissioner Gisèle Gowans and his aide-de-camp at the most respectable hotel left in Monrovia. Much to our extreme embarrassment, when we reached the check-in desk we were told that a mistake had been made and the rooms for the general had been given to a Chinese diplomatic delegation that had arrived earlier in the day. We had no choice but to book them into a very ordinary couple of rooms which were several flights up, and for which there was no working lift. They were very gracious about this and took it in their stride.

Less than two hours later the general faced the full thrust of the Liberian media, including representatives from all the major newspapers as well as two television channels. Later that evening the interview was being shown on the nation's T.V. stations and repeated several times.

Salvationists quite rightly felt this was a great start to the general's visit to Liberia. It was an impressive interview which gave The Salvation Army a much greater profile in Liberia and a recognition that we were there to stay. I was doubly happy, because at the same time news was reaching us that the rebels had been driven back from their positions at St. Paul Bridge. There seemed to be very little likelihood now that they would enter Monrovia during the general's visit.

A council for all the officers and cadets, with 45 delegates, was held and the general later said in his report; "*The testimonies could have been lifted straight out of the pages of the Acts of the Apostles.*" One of the highlights of the general's visit was the opening of the new Len Millar School, which included the unveiling of a plaque. However, behind the scenes there was a drama going on that the general knew nothing of until he was about to leave. On the site of our new school building there was a large warehouse, which we did not destroy when we developed the site. Instead we put a roof on it, so that it could become an indoor basketball court. It was in this auditorium where we held the opening ceremony with the general, his wife, the Minister of Education and various other dignitaries in attendance. Unknown to me, the property manager, David Bainda had in the morning, noticed that several cracks had appeared on the walls of the building, and it was possible the walls of the building would not hold the weight of the roof for long. With the influx of about eight hundred people into the building it was possible the whole structure could cave in.

Later, David told me he prayed hard that it would survive the celebrations, but he also added; "*I wondered if the walls did begin to collapse, where would my duty lie; whom should I attempt to rescue first, the General or his wife?*"

Fortunately it never came to that! Everything went off exceedingly well and the General declared the school to be "*without question, the smartest building in Monrovia.*" The Minister of Education, Evelyn Kandakai, was also fulsome in her praise of both the school and the work The Salvation Army was doing for the young people of Liberia in the field of education. Work began at the gym to put in place extra supporting columns as soon as the general departed from the country.

General John Larsson

In 2003 insurgents once again managed to enter Monrovia from St. Paul Bridge district, and almost took control of the whole city. The entire Bushrod Island sector was taken and the insurgents were only halted when they reached the 'New Bridge', as it is called by Monrovians. Taylor had stretched his forces too far - he had allowed some of them to penetrate into the Ivory Coast. He was now fighting MODEL in the east and trying to hold LURD at bay to the north-west. He was so desperate for fighters at this stage that some of his people were driving around in pickups trying to grab youths off the streets of Monrovia to take them to the front. It was a dangerous time for our hostel boys. Several had very narrow escapes as they jumped over fences and ran through gardens to avoid capture.

Then came the dramatic news on August 2; Charles Taylor had agreed to step down and enter exile in Nigeria. Gyude Bryant was then installed as temporary National Chairman. With this the rebels agreed to end their fighting. Hallelujah!

This meant that when General Larsson arrived in April 2004 the country was enjoying a time of relative peace, and was the first of our international leaders to be able to travel outside Greater Monrovia. The church building at Salala had just been completed, along with a school, so we took the general forty miles out to Salala, on the Gbarnga Road, to see the buildings and to unveil a plaque, naming the school after his predecessor: the 'John Gowans School'.

Funds for the building had been provided by students from a school in Norway. I felt a bit embarrassed because there weren't many church members present; they had all headed off into Monrovia for the Congress celebrations that were to be held with the general that afternoon in Monrovia. I should have thought of that.

The visit of General Larsson followed on from another significant event in the progress of The Salvation Army as a permanently established entity in Liberia; we bought the former Russian embassy. This was something that once again we owe to the generosity of Tony Hage. The embassy was on half an acre with one three-storey building, one two-bedroom bungalow and several outhouses. It was known that other parties had been eager to obtain it to convert it into a hotel/night club but immediately it came on the market Tony informed us. He could have been the agent for one of the others seeking to buy it and made a considerable amount for himself, but his admiration for The Salvation Army meant he allowed us to have first refusal on the purchase without seeking a large commission for himself. As a Command we did not have the US$150,000, but after one telephone call to the General's office in London the cash was promised and we went ahead and bought the property. We saw this not only as a victory for The Salvation Army, but also of Christianity over communism.

Interestingly, a week after we had exchanged contracts on the building a Russian government official came to reclaim their property. Fortunately, all documentation had been thoroughly checked before signing and their lease had run out several months previously.

It was therefore very fitting that the general who had ensured that we could purchase the building was with us to perform the opening ceremony and unveil a commemorative plaque. Though a great deal of work was still needed to make the building ready for full use as our HQ and the bungalow renovated to be in a fit state for us to live in, the potential of the whole compound was clear for him to see. We were able to explain the vision we had for the property, which not only included all the Command administrative offices but also for the top floor to house a short-term residency for the extension training courses. Added to this, we envisaged at least two apartments being made available for visiting personnel. By the time we left Liberia most of this was achieved.

I believe the general left Liberia knowing that he had played a positive role in the onward progress of The Salvation Army's work in Liberia.

Flying out of Liberia was often not very straight-forward. The biggest problem was that the smaller airlines often came at the wrong time or didn't arrive at all. On one occasion we had to take a visiting auditor to the airport three times on three different days before her plane arrived. When we took General Larsson and his wife to the airport we waited for a time before we were informed that his flight to Ghana, the first leg of his journey to London, was cancelled. This was a big problem because he had to take a flight for an official visit to Italy the following day. However, we discovered there was a small plane arriving soon that was going to Abidjan, and that he could catch flights from there to get him home in time. Once again Tony came to our aid, using his contacts in Abidjan to get the general's party seats on a plane to London that same day. Remarkably, they arrived back in London a little earlier than they would have done if all had gone according to the pre-arranged plans.

To have three international Salvation Army leaders visit a small Command in seven years was probably quite unusual, and though the visits were very brief they gave great encouragement to this new expression of salvationism. I think the generals themselves were also encouraged by what they saw and heard with their own eyes and ears when, to quote General Gowans, they met this 'positively unique' Army.

We were very grateful to all of them for the way they accepted, without complaint, the lack of usual comforts assigned to international leaders. Each of them gave the Command much encouragement and a vision of the future for The Salvation Army in Liberia.

CHAPTER 17

In Conclusion

The Salvation Army had a rule for which very few exceptions were made; that all male officers, apart from the general, have to retire when they reach the age of 65 years. Nevertheless, we did seek to become one of those few exceptions and requested another two years in Liberia.

The foundations for the construction of the Vocational College on the site opposite the Municipal City Hall had just been finished. We had hoped that we would be permitted to stay long enough see it finished and that I should be able to set up the first set programmes, syllabuses and timetables for the college. This was not to be, and though we were disappointed we were grateful for having been trusted for thirteen challenging years to be pioneers for The Salvation Army and proclaimers of the Gospel in Liberia. I'm thankful too that no one had drawn attention to the fact that Dorothy, being five and a half years older than me, was halfway through her 70th year before she retired with me.

Plans were made for our farewell from Liberia. Salvationists were to come from all over Liberia to say goodbye to us on the last Sunday before our departure from the country, but the full pleasure of that event was to be denied us.

In the early hours of our final Sunday trouble broke out between two groups in the Paynesville part of greater Monrovia, and the outcome was a conflict between Christian and Muslim youths. Quickly the origin of the complaint became very obscure, as mosques and churches were looted and set ablaze. This happened just a few days after Major and Mrs Dixon had arrived to replace us; quite a shock for them! They had understood that the fighting in the city had ended.

This really had little or no connection with the factional fighting that had been going on for nearly the length of our time in Liberia, though the young men involved probably included some former combatants. We began to fear for our churches and even our schools, as the trouble seemed to be spiralling out of control.

Then there was sound of an angry mob coming our way, and all we could do was to lock our gates and wait. Our two security guards were only school graduates who would stand no chance of defending us, or the building. if the compound was attacked. But the mob passed us by and went to the mosque that had been built between our new HQ and our former one. These were not Christians who were beating the night watchman and tearing the roof of the mosque – they were looters, pure and simple, using the initial trouble to give them grounds to pilfer and destroy the mosque. They even tried to burn it before they left. This kind of activity was happening all over the city. Clearly something had to be done. The Peacekeepers moved in and cordoned off large parts of the city.

There was now no way our farewell service could take place as planned. We couldn't get to Paynesville Church where it was to be held and even if we switched the service to the City Church which we could get to, very few Salvationists from other corps, including those who had travelled in from outside of Monrovia, would not be able to get there because of the roadblocks. We waited as long as possible to see if the emergency restrictions would be lifted, but in the end a decision was made to hold two services: one for most of the people (but not us) at Paynesville and another one (with us) at City Corps.

This was a complete anti-climax to our departure, but we had no choice. The few days that followed saw a continuous procession of visitors to HQ to present their token offerings and offer their simple verbal tributes to us. We shall never forget the tears that were shed on those occasions particularly from members of the girls' hostel and those from more senior personnel like Lieutenant Momo Duwee and Captain Garmai Davis.

When the day of departure came, as many Salvationists as could find any transport travelled along to send us off. We didn't linger outside the airport, or else we too would have shown the tears that were in our eyes. We shook all their hands and then, accompanied by David Bainda, went into the airport with a final turn and wave. Hugging and saying good bye to our adopted son, Ernest, was especially emotional, for we didn't know for sure that we would ever see him again. The British Embassy had made it clear that Ernest would not be granted a visa to visit us. We had never wanted Ernest to come to the UK permanently, but we had obtained a sponsorship for him to attend the London School of Theology and thought that he would return to Liberia better able to contribute to the spiritual growth of The Salvation Army in his own country.

Now, more than five years later he still has not been able to get to the UK but after two years we were able to visit him in Liberia. Since leaving him, Liberia's cell phone companies have worked surprisingly well and even the internet is now working on most days so we are happy that we have been able to keep in constant touch with him. He has progressed from being assistant accountant at The Salvation Army HQ to Paymaster for the aid agency 'Africare', and is now the senior accountant at JSI Research and Training Institute in Monrovia. He is still active in the City Corps of The Salvation Army.

Of course, we still had our grown-up family back home that were looking forward to seeing more of us. We have three children in England, Malcolm, Graham and Helen. Each has their own family, and so we would now be able to see much more of our grandchildren and great-grandchildren (of whom there were already quite a few).

We are happy to say that each of them has retained their links with The Salvation Army: Malcolm as an officer at Ivybridge, near Plymouth, Graham as a soldier at Dunstable and Helen as an adherent at Tunbridge Wells. We had not yet decided where we were going to soldier in retirement.

Once we had climbed into the plane and found our seats, we settled down for the long and usually boring flight. This trip, however, was to be a little different. As always we were travelling in our Salvation Army uniforms, and this attracted the attention of a stewardess. For the next hour, whenever she was free, the stewardess returned to talk with us about our work and our faith. This was not a shallow conversation, for she was deeply interested to know how we felt about God in our lives. It was just like the conversation Jesus had with Nicodemus; she was clearly searching for spiritual truth, and we felt privileged to have had the chance to share our personal faith with her.

As we continued our flight home, it was not easy to come to terms with the fact that we could be leaving Africa for the last time. We were sad, but satisfied that we had been true to our convictions and calling during our time in Liberia. We had seen tremendous growth in the educational and medical work of The Salvation Army, but each of these activities had been well used to promote our primary aim - to grow the church; in numbers and in spiritual depth. We had seen the Holy Spirit working in a wonderful way and rejoiced that guns, rockets, bombs and diseases - as well as all forms of intimidation - had not prevented us fulfilling our calling from God to Liberia. We had proclaimed the Gospel and sought to disciple the converted, whilst ministering to human needs in a holistic way. We had been given the tremendous privilege to help build the Kingdom of God in Liberia and to see our ministry bear glorious fruit!

May the work of The Salvation Army, together with all true churches in Liberia, continue to flourish - **and to God be the Glory!**

APPENDIX 1

Churches in Liberia

The strongest and the most emboldened to speak out against the atrocities of war and corruption at every level was the **Roman Catholic Church**. Their leader, Bishop Francis, was a thorn in the side of Charles Taylor until the Bishop had a stroke that left him totally incapacitated and unable to speak.

Generally R. C. schools, of which there were many throughout the country, were the least corrupt and most respected. In Monrovia, for most of the time we were in Liberia, their hospital was the only place which had the equipment, medicines and qualified personal that could justify the name 'hospital'. The Catholics have to be admired for the way, time after time, they went back into the interior to rebuild their schools and clinics. During the time we were around we knew of several places that were rebuilt at least three times. Father Lee and Sister Barbara were really brave people who we were happy to call friends.

The first President of Liberia, J.J. Roberts, had been a **Methodist,** so various strands of that denomination were also prominent. They owned much of the most valuable land in the capital. They also had schools and medical facilities, though their hospital at Ganta was in the hands of the rebels for a lot of the time. Their university in Monrovia has been brought up to a credible standard since the ending of the civil conflict.

Cuttington University belonged to the **Episcopalian Church,** and when it was brought back into operation it was accepted as easily the best university in the country. Not far from there, Phebe hospital was also of a high standard when allowed to function properly, but being in the path of the rebel's advance on Monrovia, it was time and again looted and partially destroyed.

Other active churches in the educational and medical field included the **Seventh Day Adventists** and to a lesser extent the **Lutherans**, **Baptists** and a variety of **Pentecostal Churches.** Another hospital and clinic close to Monrovia which performed a valuable service, when not being affected by rebel activity, was **ELWA** (Eternal Love Winning Africa). Their expatriate doctors and nurses were treated very roughly by NPFL fighters in the 1996 attack on Monrovia, but they were quick to start operating their clinic again once the fighting died down. They also operate a religious radio station.

APPENDIX 2

"Taylor Must Go"

Below is a true reproduction of a flyer that was being spread about as the forces of LURD began to get closer to overcoming President Taylor's militia in 2002. Fortunately there never was much support for an Islamic Republic in Liberia and even when LURD forced Taylor to go into exile and a provisional government was set up, the concept of Shari Law was never mentioned.

TAYLOR MUST GO!

Our Fellow Muslims Brothers and Sisters, ALLAH IS GREAT!!

Our successful attack on the Klay Junction on the 8th day of this month marks the turning point in our Holy War against the infidels of the Charles Taylor Government. For over five years now, we have demanded an equal share of the Government with the Christians but Mr. Taylor refused. We have a right as natives of Liberia to enjoy the Liberian government but from time to time, Mr. Taylor ignored us and sidelined us. We have no alternative but to fight. This Islamic Jihad is ordained by Allah. Our mission is clear: to overthrow the commander of the infidels, Mr. Charles Taylor and his advisor, Rev. Michael Francis of the Catholic Church so as to set up an Islamic state in Liberia that will strictly adhere to the principles of Shari a law.

In the name of Allah, the Islamic Jihad movement of LURD is congratulating all its followers for adhering to koranic teachings. We condemn those complacent Muslims in Liberia who are advocating the co-existence of Muslims and Christians. We will resist with our blood any co-existence of Muslims and Christians in Liberia. Since churches are symbols of sinful worship, we urge our followers to burn them down now! This is the command of Allah.

Charles Taylor may describe us a terrorists but we are not terrorists in the sight of Allah. The blood of the infidels at Klay is a clear indication of our determination to fight back in the face of suppression of Muslims by Mr Taylor. Our mosques in Monrovia have been burnt by Taylor soldiers and when we enter Monrovia, they will pay with their blood. The blood of the infidels and others to follow in subsequent attacks will be to the glorification of Allah. The Koran teaches that it is not a sin for Muslims not to possess weapons that will prevent the Christians from inflicting harm on Muslims.

Our strategy is guerrilla warfare aimed at bringing death to those that disobeyed the edict of the Prophet Mohammed. Mr. Taylor says he wrote the book in guerrilla warfare but when infidel blood begins to spill on the streets of Monrovia, he would realize that Allah is Great!

LIBERIAN UNITED FOR RECONCILIATION AND DEMOCRACY(LURD) - February 2002

APPENDIX 3

Jonathan Hart – A Brief Autobiography

My late father was a native of Nigeria. Born 1926. he studied in the United States of America and came to Liberia upon the request of the Liberian Government for medical practitioners.

His wife came with him, but she was barren and bore him no children. After several years of unsuccessful medical trials she allowed him to take another woman who could bare him children.

According to him, this was a family agreement. Altogether my father took three different women, including my biological mother, who was from Bomi County.

The second woman bore him two children, a girl and a boy.

My mother was his third wife and on April 17 1976 she gave birth to his son. Later, on September 11 1981, she gave birth to me and my twin brother.

Our birth was a problem-packed situation because our mother carried the pregnancy for more than nine months. This caused her father to go to a native doctor to find out the cause of the prolonged pregnancy. That doctor told him that there were two children in my mother's womb, but the smaller one was trying to kill her, his parent, and there was a war going on between the two children. Therefore, if she should give birth to both of them, the smaller oneshould not be allowed to live because if he did he would still try to kill his parents.

Things happened as predicted by the native doctor in that my mother gave birth to twins - myself and my brother. My mother's family requested my father to perform the ritual killing, but he refused. Because he refused to kill the smaller child, they insisted that their daughter - my mother - return to their family home with them. Since then I have not seen her, nor any other member of her family.

This happened three weeks after our birth but our father only told us just before he was executed. Until that time we lived with our father and step-mother believing her to be our biological mother.

In July 1990 our parents were arrested on their farm in Grand Cape Mount County, by NPFL rebels, for being government workers and Nigerian. They were then taken to a camp in Bomi Hills where they were kept alongside many other foreign nationals from Guinea, Ghana. and Sierra Leone. It was then that they told me the person I had always known as my mother was not my mother.

On a daily basis the rebels selected any they chose to kill from among their captives and then executed them. In October 1990 my parents were beheaded, and we were also hunted to be killed. It was the custom that once the parents were killed all other family members should be killed as well.

During this time a lady took me and ran with me to neighbouring Sierra Leone, where I remained until the civil war broke out there in 1991. This situation brought me back to Liberia, where I was arrested on suspicion of being a member of the fighting group in Sierra Leone. While in prison, Mr. Nelson Taylor - the older brother of Charles Taylor - visited the prison and requested that I be released. He took me to live with him. I remained with him but refused to become a child soldier, on the grounds that I could not join others to kill people because of what I was going through as a result of the murder of my own parents.

After Octopus - the famous battle to capture Monrovia - in 1992, I came to Monrovia where I met my half-sister. She took me in her home and for some time we were friends. But later things turned bad for both of us. During my time with her I sold garrie and other food stuff in the street for the survival of the family, and did all other menial jobs in the home. It was difficult living with her as she never wanted me to go to church, nor have any recreation with other kids.

Through all these times I remained committed to my God, and was always praying for intervention. At the appropriate time God came in and saved my future. I met The Salvation Army, and my future was put on track.

I will become a doctor and serve God, and work to promote the health of all people.

Only by God's grace am I alive today - **for I was the youngest twin!**

APPENDIX 4

Glossary of Salvation Army Terms

General	Head of the international Salvation Army
Captain, Major, Lt. Colonel, Colonel Commissioner & General	Ordained Salvation Army Ministers known as '**Officers**'
Corps	Salvation Army Church(es)
Commissioning	Ordination
Lieutenants*/Envoys	Corps Leaders who have not attended the OTC
Cadet	A man or woman training to become an officer
Officer Training College/(O.T.C.)	Seminary
Training Principal	Officer in-charge of the Seminary/(O.T.C.)
Soldier	A converted person 14+ who has signed 'A Soldiers Covenant' and become a full member of The Salvation Army.

* 'Lieutenant' In the future this rank is used only for Commissioned and Ordained officers.

Junior Soldier	A converted boy or girl who has accepted Jesus as their Saviour, has signed the Junior Soldiers promise and become a junior member of The Salvation Army
Corps Sergeant Major (CSM)	Elder of the Corps who oversights services and is usually the church leader when there is no other appointed leader.
League of Mercy	A group of Salvationists who visit prisoners, hospitals and those in need to offer the gospel message along side practical assistance